www.themailbo

The Mailbox® Monthly Idea Books—
Your Ultimate Monthly Resource!

Your friends at *The Mailbox*® have taken monthly books to a whole new level! We've created a Web site that contains even more classroom resources to complement the hundreds of curriculum-based activities in each book. We've also added skill lines to each idea for a quick curriculum reference at a glance. Plus, every book has a comprehensive index to make planning and selecting activities even easier! All of these terrific features make this series of monthly books one that you can't be without!

Now Internet Interactive!

- For each book, you'll enjoy over **50 pages** of online resources, such as patterns, reproducibles, transparency masters, and classroom forms!
- You'll find **new** resources for **every** thematic unit in each book!
- Many classroom forms can be **filled out online** and printed. No more handwritten versions!
- Web site content is tailored to you and your **grade level.**
- **All** reproducibles and pattern pages from each monthly book are available online for **easy printing.**
- Access is absolutely **FREE!**

Getting your online extras
is as easy as 1, 2, 3!

1. Go to www.themailboxbooks.com and click on "Add a book."
2. Complete the simple registration form.
3. Follow the on-screen instructions to add your book.

**Look for the computer icon 🖥️
throughout each book to guide you to
your FREE online extras.**

About This Book

It's hard to believe we could improve on our best-selling series of monthly idea books—but we have! In this edition, you'll find the following exciting new features added to our irreplaceable collection of curriculum-based ideas!

- A Web site containing *even more* classroom resources complements the hundreds of activities provided in each book. (To access this incredible site for free, follow the simple instructions found on page 1.)
- A skill line for each idea provides a curriculum reference at a glance.
- A comprehensive index makes selecting and planning activities a breeze!

We think you'll agree that these new features make this series of monthly books the best ever!

Managing Editors: Cayce Guiliano, Deborah T. Kalwat, Scott Lyons
Editor at Large: Diane Badden
Contributing Writers: Patricia Altmann, Irving P. Crump, Kelly Gooden, Peggy W. Hambright, Simone Lepine, Elizabeth H. Lindsay, Debra Liverman, Thad H. McLaurin, Cindy Mondello, Marsha Schmus, Judith Shutter, Mary Spaulding, Elizabeth Tanzi, Irene Taylor, Christine A. Thuman, Stephanie Willett-Smith, Pat Wimberley
Copy Editors: Sylvan Allen, Lynn Bemer Coble, Gina Farago, Karen Brewer Grossman, Karen L. Huffman, Amy Kirtley-Hill, Laurel Robinson, Jennifer Rudisill, Debbie Shoffner
Cover Artist: Clevell Harris
Art Coordinator: Theresa Lewis Goode
Artists: Jennifer T. Bennett, Pam Crane, Theresa Lewis Goode, Nick Greenwood, Clevell Harris, Ivy L. Koonce, Sheila Krill, Rob Mayworth, Clint Moore, Greg D. Rieves, Rebecca Saunders, Barry Slate, Donna K. Teal
Typesetters: Lynette Dickerson, Mark Rainey
Indexer: Elizabeth Findley Caran
The Mailbox® Books.com: Kimberley Bruck (manager); Debra Liverman, Sharon Murphy (associate editors); Jennifer L. Tipton (designer/artist); Troy Lawrence, Stuart Smith (production artists); Karen White (editorial assistant); Paul Fleetwood, Xiaoyun Wu (systems)

President, The Mailbox Book Company™: Joseph C. Bucci
Director of Book Planning and Development: Chris Poindexter
Book Development Managers: Elizabeth H. Lindsay, Thad McLaurin, Susan Walker
Curriculum Director: Karen P. Shelton
Traffic Manager: Lisa K. Pitts
Librarian: Dorothy C. McKinney
Editorial and Freelance Management: Karen A. Brudnak
Editorial Training: Irving P. Crump
Editorial Assistants: Terrie Head, Hope Rodgers, Jan E. Witcher

Manufactured in the United States
10 9 8 7 6 5 4 3 2 1

APRIL
Table of Contents

April Calendar

National Garden Month

In observance of National Garden Month, invite a local horticulturist to share some gardening tips with your class. Afterward, have your students put these tips to good use around your school by weeding and mulching garden beds. Finally, plant new flowers to make the school a more beautiful place.

Prevention of Animal Cruelty Month

April is Prevention of Animal Cruelty Month. This month focuses our attention on the proper care of animals. Have your class sponsor a schoolwide canned pet-food drive. Donate the proceeds of the food drive to your local humane society. Your students will feel proud of their efforts to help the animals in your community.

1—April Fools' Day

Most everyone has been the victim of an April Fools' Day joke, yet few know the origins of this unusual day. Centuries ago the Romans celebrated New Year's Day in spring with an eight-day celebration that began on March 25 and ended on April 1. When King Charles IX changed the calendar, April 1 was no longer New Year's Day. Many people did not adjust to this confusing change. The pranks and tricks played on April 1 mark the old New Year's Day. Discuss how we would celebrate New Year's Day if King Charles IX had not changed the calendar.

2—International Children's Book Day

International Children's Book Day, which commemorates children's literature from around the world, is held each year on the birthday of Hans Christian Andersen. Have each student celebrate this day by sharing his favorite children's book with a younger student.

3—The First Ride of the Pony Express

The Pony Express made its debut on this day in 1860. Its route stretched across the United States and had 153 mail stations. At each station new riders and fresh horses waited to continue the 1,900-mile journey. Mail normally arrived at its destination in less than 7 1/2 days. Have each student imagine one day in the life of a Pony Express rider. Direct the student to write a journal entry detailing the adventures of that day.

6—Anniversary of First Modern Olympic Games

On April 6, 1896, Athens, Greece, hosted the first modern Olympic Games. Thirteen countries participated in nine sports: wrestling, weight lifting, track and field, swimming, shooting, lawn tennis, gymnastics, fencing, and cycling. Challenge each student to research and list the sports that were showcased in the most recent Olympic Games.

10—U.S. Patent System Established

The U.S. patent system was established on this date in 1790. A patent ensures that an inventor has the exclusive rights to her idea. Have each student research one invention. Have her record in her journal the inventor, the name of the invention, when it was first patented, and the expiration date of the patent.

15—Birthday of Leonardo da Vinci

Leonardo da Vinci, the famous scientist, inventor, and artist, was born on this day in 1452. Leonardo's most famous artistic works include the *Mona Lisa* and *The Last Supper*. Many of Leonardo's inventions and scientific ideas were years ahead of his time. Have each student select one of Leonardo's masterpieces, scientific observations, or inventions to research. Then direct the student to give an oral report on the selected topic.

24—First American Newspaper Published

Postmaster John Campbell published the first American newspaper, *The Boston News-Letter,* on this date in 1704. Newspapers help keep us informed about local, state, national, and world events. Have your class create its own newspaper to keep parents up-to-date on the happenings at school.

26—Birthday of John James Audubon

John James Audubon was born on this day in 1785. He is known for his field research involving North American birds and other wildlife. A collection of over 1,065 of his sketches and detailed notes was eventually published in the book *Birds of America*. Challenge each student to go on a bird-watching expedition of his own and draw quick sketches of the birds he observes. Have the student share his sketches in class. Then combine the sketches to create a class anthology of birds.

FREE-TIME FUN for April!

Tackle these 20 terrific tasks when you finish your work.

Monday	Tuesday	Wednesday	Thursday	Friday
April is Keep America Beautiful Month. List four things you could do around your school to help make it a more beautiful place.	Pay tribute to a volunteer in your school by writing that person a thank-you note.	April is National Humor Month. Explain what the saying "laughter is the best medicine" means.	National Library Week is celebrated in April. Make a list of your five favorite books.	The word *spring* names a season, but it also has other meanings. Use the dictionary to find at least two other meanings for spring. Record and illustrate the meanings.
April 1 is April Fools' Day. List some of the jokes that have been played on you on this day.	Make a pictograph showing the hair color of your classmates. Brown Black Blonde	April is Prevention of Animal Cruelty Month. Name five ways you could help animals.	Draw five signs of spring.	On April 29, 1913, Gideon Sandback received a patent for the zipper. List all of the items you can think of that use a zipper.
In 1902, it cost ten cents to go to a movie. Find the difference between the present-day cost of a movie and the cost in 1902.	National Garden Month is in April. Name three foods you enjoy eating that come from a garden.	Write your first name vertically on a sheet of paper. Next to each letter, write one adjective to describe yourself. Jolly Artistic Kind Educated	On April 15, 1770, the eraser was invented. Keep track of how many times you use your eraser today.	Design a new type of back-pack for students.
Astronomy Day is observed in April. Draw the outline of a major constellation.	April is National Automobile Month. Design the car you will be driving in the year 2050. How is it different from your parents' car?	Public Schools Week is celebrated in April. List six ways your life would be different if you did not attend school.	In honor of Fresh Florida Tomato Month, draw six foods that contain tomatoes.	List five ways you could make your home a safer place.

©The Education Center, Inc. • APRIL • TEC209

Note to the teacher: Have each student staple a copy of this page inside a file folder. Direct students to store their completed work inside their folders.

Desktag: Duplicate student copies on construction paper. Have each student personalize and decorate his pattern; then laminate the patterns and use them as desktags during April.

Award: Make multiple copies. Keep them handy at your desk during the month of April. When a student earns an award, write his name, the subject, the date, and your signature on the appropriate lines. Special prizes can be given with the awards.

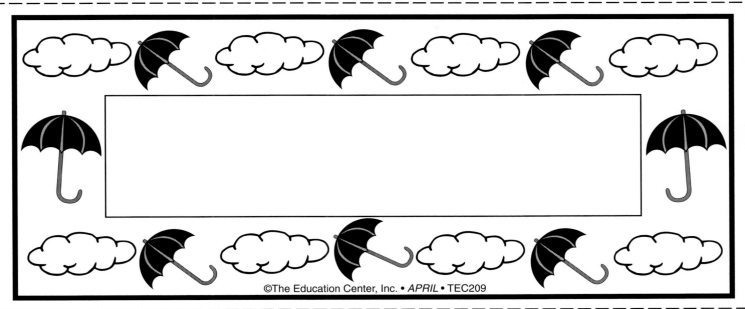

©The Education Center, Inc. • *APRIL* • TEC209

IS

MAKING A
SPLASH IN

Presented _____ day
this _____ of April for

OUTSTANDING
WORK!

Teacher

©The Education Center, Inc. • *APRIL* • TEC209

We've Got the Whole Earth in Our Hands

First celebrated on April 22, 1970, Earth Day continues to remind us to "Give Earth a Chance." Use the following activities to help students understand and appreciate the importance of protecting our earth and all of its wonderful resources.

by Cindy Mondello and Thad McLaurin

The Global Gazette 💻
Writing for a variety of purposes, making a personal connection

During your Earth Day unit, have each student keep a journal of his thoughts and feelings about various environmental topics. Duplicate the journal cover on page 15 for each student. Have each student create his journal by stapling the cover to 20 sheets of notebook paper. Provide each student with markers or crayons to decorate his cover page.

Suggested journal topics to get your students started:

- Is your town or city experiencing pollution problems? What are they? Make a list of possible solutions to the problems.
- Close your eyes and picture yourself in a special place surrounded by nature. Where are you? What sounds do you hear? What do you see? How does this place make you feel?
- You are an alien from a distant planet, and you have just landed on the earth. Describe the things you like best about this planet.
- Pretend you are Mother Earth. Write a letter urging humans to protect the environment. Suggest ways that humans can help preserve the earth.
- Why is it important to recycle?
- Illustrate a bumper sticker with a catchy, but meaningful, environmental message.
- We are rapidly running out of landfill space. What are some ways people can decrease the amount of garbage they produce each day?
- Oil spills have caused much destruction along our shores. How can future oil spills be prevented?
- Your best friend just threw his soda can out the car window. How do you handle this situation?

Acid Rain—Silent but Deadly

Conducting an experiment,
understanding the effects of acid rain

Cars and coal-burning electric-power plants spew pollutants into the atmosphere where they are chemically changed into *acid rain*. Acid rain erodes buildings and destroys plants and animals. Demonstrate the effects of acid rain by placing a piece of chalk in a glass jar containing vinegar. Tell students that the acidic vinegar eating away at the chalk is similar to acid rain slowly eroding buildings. Next, recruit student volunteers to help test the effects of acid rain on plants.

Materials: 2 small plants, water, vinegar, 2 plastic containers

Directions:

Step 1: Mix three cups of water and one cup of vinegar in a plastic container. Label this container "Acid Rain."

Step 2: Fill the other container with four cups of water. Label this container "Water."

Step 3: Label one plant "Acid Rain" and one plant "Water."

Step 4: Water each plant every three days for two weeks, using equal amounts of liquid from the appropriate containers.

Step 5: At the end of two weeks, have the students describe the two plants. Then ask the students, "What do you think happens to an entire forest when acid rain falls on it week after week?"

The plant watered with the acid rain mixture will be limp and the leaves will turn brown. The plant receiving only water will be healthy and strong.

Trash Troopers

Collecting, graphing, and interpreting data

One of the biggest ways people pollute the environment is by dropping "stuff" on the ground that does not belong there. It's called littering. Help your students learn more about litter and clean up your school's campus at the same time with the following activity. Divide students into teams of three or four. Supply each team with one copy of the reproducible on page 16, a trash bag, rubber gloves, a marker, and several sheets of newspaper. Review the directions and rules for trash collecting on page 16. Then assign each team a specific area of the school grounds. Tell each team to spend 15 minutes collecting trash in its assigned area and then meet back at a designated location to complete the rest of the activity. Have each team follow the directions on page 16 for sorting and graphing its trash. Conclude the activity by having each team present its litter graph to the rest of the class.

A Rotten Recipe
Conducting an experiment, understanding decomposition

Teach your students how to reduce, reuse, and recycle all at the same time by making *compost*—an organic fertilizer. Recruit a parent volunteer to construct a 4' x 4' wooden bin with a removable top. Set the box on a level area of your schoolyard. Place fresh straw in the bottom. Have students save salad, fruit, vegetable, and bread scraps from their lunches. Also ask the cafeteria staff to save eggshells for the compost. Do not add dairy products, meats, or fats to the bin. Cover the scraps with a thin layer of soil and a layer of grass or weed clippings. Continue the process of building layer upon layer. *Aerate,* or get air into, the compost by turning the scraps and soil over with a shovel or pitchfork each week. If desired, add earthworms to the compost to speed up the breakdown of the materials. Keep the compost moist, but cover it if heavy rain is forecast. In four to six weeks, the compost will be ready to spread around trees and shrubbery. Also, mix it with the soil in planting beds on the school grounds. Keep up the rotten work!

Trash Town, USA
Researching the causes and effects of pollution, problem solving

Tell your students they have just become citizens of Trash Town, USA. Some very serious pollution problems are threatening the town. Divide the students into four "Pollution Preventing Teams." Duplicate the reproducible on page 17. Cut along the dotted lines and give each team a different "Pollution Problem Card." Have each team research the questions on its problem card. Then instruct each group to develop a plan to solve or correct the pollution problem. Have each group present its problem, its research, and its plan of action to the rest of the class. Encourage the class to suggest other actions to help solve the pollution problems.

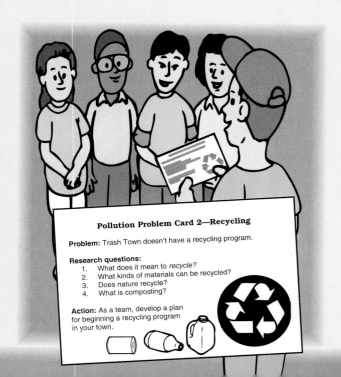

Pollution Problem Card 2—Recycling

Problem: Trash Town doesn't have a recycling program.

Research questions:
1. What does it mean to *recycle?*
2. What kinds of materials can be recycled?
3. Does nature recycle?
4. What is composting?

Action: As a team, develop a plan for beginning a recycling program in your town.

Garbage Galore
Conducting an experiment, understanding decomposition

The average American produces about three pounds of trash each day. That's a lot of trash! Where does it all go, and what happens to it once it gets there? Many food wastes and some kinds of paper quickly break down, or *decompose,* and help make the soil richer. However, other wastes do not decompose quickly and just keep piling up.

Use the following activity to help your students determine the types of waste that decompose quickly. Enlist several students to fill four large buckets with dirt. Moisten the dirt with water. Then bury one of the following items in each bucket: a banana peel, a piece of paper, a piece of aluminum foil, and a plastic bag. Label each bucket according to its item. After a week, have students dig up each item and record what has happened to it. Then rebury the items. Repeat this process for four or five weeks. Have students conclude from the experiment which items were *biodegradable* (decomposed quickly) and which were not. Encourage students to explain how this experiment has helped them be more selective in what they throw away.

Pollution Puzzle: Black Death Strikes Europe!
Critical thinking, participating in an oral presentation

Around 1350 the bubonic plague, or black death, struck Europe. Nearly half of Europe's population died as a result. The plague was spread by rats and fleas. Fleas fed on the blood of infected rats and then transferred the ingested plague bacteria to humans through flea bites.

Before you tell students the real cause of the bubonic plague, have them work in critical-thinking groups to construct a theory explaining the cause of the plague. Make six copies of pages 18 and 19. Cut apart each set of clues from page 19 and place it in a separate envelope. Divide the students into six groups and give each group one envelope of clues, a copy of page 18, one sheet of chart paper, and a set of markers. Instruct each group to read the assignment and procedures on page 18 and to read each clue in its envelope. Then give each group 15 minutes to determine the cause of the bubonic plague. Next, instruct each group to spend about 15 minutes illustrating its theory on the chart paper. Have each group present its theory and illustration to the rest of the class. End with a discussion revealing the actual cause of the plague.

YODELAYDEE... WHEW!

Earth-Smart Cleaners

*Understanding the effects of human behaviors
on the environment*

Television commercials have familiarized students with the latest bathroom and kitchen cleaners and furniture polishes. But most students aren't aware that many cleaning products are harmful to the environment. Send home the following environmentally safe cleaner recipes for your students and their families to make and use.

Earth-Smart Glass Cleaner:
Mix four tablespoons of vinegar with four cups of water in an empty spray bottle. Spray on any type of glass and wipe dry with a clean cloth.
©The Education Center, Inc.

Earth-Smart Bathroom and Kitchen Cleaner:
Use baking soda to clean the kitchen sink and counters as well as the bathroom tub and tile. Rinse well with water and wipe dry with a clean cloth.
©The Education Center, Inc.

Earth-Smart Furniture Cleaner:
Combine one cup of water with one cup of lemon juice in an empty spray bottle. Spray a clean cloth; then wipe the furniture clean. Keep refrigerated when not in use.
©The Education Center, Inc.

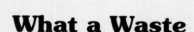

What a Waste

*Understanding the effects of human behaviors
on the environment, critical thinking*

Have you ever bought something that had so much packaging you ended up throwing away as much as you kept? Packaging makes a product look more attractive and helps to hold items together, but often a lot of unneeded layers are used. For example, a box of chocolates may have five or six layers of packaging. All this extra packaging creates a lot of unnecessary trash. About one-third of the garbage in a landfill consists of discarded packaging.

Help your students become more informed consumers by asking each student to bring in one packaged product to analyze. Then have the student answer the following questions: Does it contain excess packaging? How can the packaging be improved? Can it be sold without packaging? Allow each student to present his product and his suggestions for improving its packaging to the class.

There's No Place Like Home

Understanding the effects of human behaviors on the environment

It's no secret that birds build their own nests. So why should we build birdhouses? Birds are losing their homes all over the world. Many birds are dying out and some have become extinct. Humans need to do all they can to protect the remaining birds on the earth.

Have each student follow the directions below for building a birdhouse while recycling trash at the same time. Hang the new homes around your school or let students take them home to hang.

Materials: class supply of half-gallon paper milk cartons, 2' thin flexible wire per person, duct tape, pencil, scissors, flat-head nails, pine straw, newspaper, brown spray paint

Directions:

Step 1: Open the top of the milk carton (both sides) and rinse well.

Step 2: Cover an area outside with newspaper. Place the milk carton on the newspaper; then carefully paint only the outside of the carton with brown spray paint. Allow it to dry thoroughly.

Step 3: Use scissors to cut a hole (about two inches in diameter) five inches below the top of the milk carton as shown.

Step 4: On the opposite side, use a pencil to make two holes (side by side) about five inches down from the top of the milk carton as shown.

Step 5: Insert one end of the wire into the left pencil hole, pull along the inside, and draw through the right pencil hole from the inside as shown.

Step 6: Pile one inch of pine straw on the bottom of the milk carton.

Step 7: Reclose the top of the milk carton into its original position and secure with duct tape.

Step 8: Find a large nearby tree. Hammer two flat-head nails side by side into the tree trunk. Hang the milk carton by wrapping both ends of the wire tightly around each nail.

Step 2   Step 3

Steps 4 and 5   Step 8

The Voice of the People
Making a personal connection, writing for a purpose

Challenge students to do the "write" thing to let others know that they are serious about the environment. The more letters that public officials receive on a particular topic, the more likely change in policies will occur. Have your class discuss some environmental issues, such as acid rain, product packaging, recycling, and the depletion of the ozone. Then have each student write one of the public officials given concerning an environmental issue. Duplicate the letters before mailing and post them on a bulletin board titled "Do the 'Write' Thing—Help the Environment." Post any responses on the board as well.

Addresses:

Senator_____
U.S. Senate
Washington, DC 20510

President of the United States
The White House
1600 Pennsylvania Ave.
Washington, DC 20500

Congressperson _____
U.S. House of Representatives
Washington, DC 20515

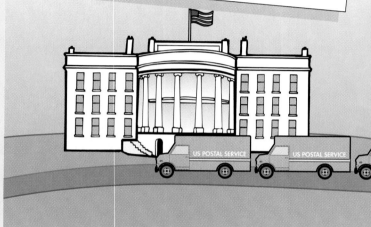

Literature Link

Looking for good resources on recycling, conservation, and the environment? The following books are helpful resources for both teacher and student:

- *Earth Book for Kids: Activities to Help Heal the Environment* by Linda Schwartz
- *Fifty Simple Things Kids Can Do to Save the Earth* by John Javna
- *Fifty Simple Things You Can Do to Save the Earth* by Earth Works Project Staff
- *Good Earth Art: Environmental Art for Kids* by MaryAnn F. Kohl
- *Taking Care of the Earth: Kids in Action* by Laurence Pringle

(Student's Name)

EARTH DAY JOURNAL

Note to the teacher: Duplicate this page for each student to use with "The Global Gazette" on page 8.

Trash Troopers to the Rescue!

Many people litter by leaving trash where it doesn't belong. Become a "Trash Trooper" and help clean up your environment. As a team, complete the activity below by following the steps provided, as well as any directions given by your teacher.

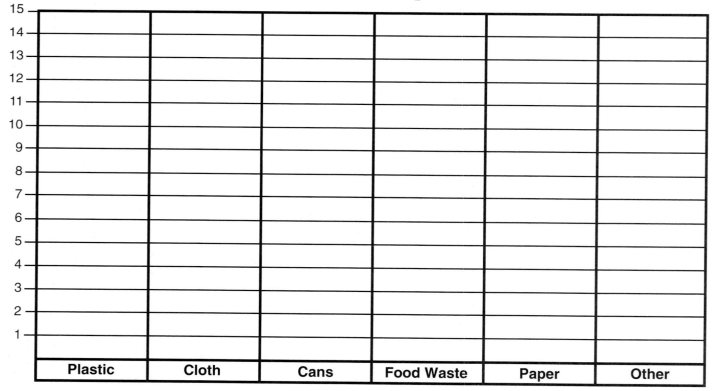

Materials:
trash bag, rubber gloves for each team member, several sheets of newspaper, marker, the graph below

Directions:

Step 1: Put on your rubber gloves. Collect litter in the area assigned by your teacher. Do not pick up any glass or other dangerous materials. Return to the area designated by the teacher in 15 minutes.

Step 2: Spread out your litter collection on the newspaper. Sort your collection into the following categories: plastic, cloth, cans, food waste, paper, and other.

Step 3: Count the number of items in each category. Use this information to complete the bar graph below.

Step 4: Present your graph to the other teams. In your presentation, recommend two or three ways litter can be decreased at your school or in the community.

Step 5: Place your litter collection back in the plastic trash bag or appropriate recycling bins. Dispose of the trash properly. Return any dry sheets of newspaper to your teacher for recycling.

Team Litter Graph

	Plastic	Cloth	Cans	Food Waste	Paper	Other
15						
14						
13						
12						
11						
10						
9						
8						
7						
6						
5						
4						
3						
2						
1						

Bonus Box: On the back of this page, list any items in your litter collection that can be recycled or reused.

Pollution Problem Card 2—Recycling

Problem: Trash Town doesn't have a recycling program.

Research questions:
1. What does it mean to *recycle?*
2. What kinds of materials can be recycled?
3. Does nature recycle?
4. What is composting?

Action: As a team, develop a plan for beginning a recycling program in your town.

©The Education Center, Inc.

Pollution Problem Card 4—Land Pollution

Problem: Trash Town's land has become polluted by garbage, litter, and industrial waste.

Research questions:
1. What are the major causes of land pollution?
2. How does land pollution contribute to water pollution?
3. How does land pollution affect plant and animal life?
4. Can polluted soil be cleaned and restored?

Action: As a team, develop a plan for cleaning up Trash Town's land and preventing further land pollution.

©The Education Center, Inc.

Pollution Problem Card 1—Air Pollution

Problem: Trash Town's factories and heavy traffic have polluted the air.

Research questions:
1. What are the main causes of air pollution?
2. What is *smog?*
3. What is currently being done to prevent air pollution in other towns?
4. How does air pollution from one country affect another country?

Action: As a team, develop a plan for decreasing the amount of air pollution in your town.

©The Education Center, Inc.

Pollution Problem Card 3—Water Pollution

Problem: Trash Town's lakes, rivers, and groundwater are polluted.

Research questions:
1. What are the main causes of water pollution?
2. How does soil contamination or land pollution affect the water supply?
3. How does water pollution affect plants and animals?
4. How have oil spills along our coasts affected the water?

Action: As a team, develop a plan for cleaning up Trash Town's water and preventing further water pollution.

©The Education Center, Inc.

Note to the teacher: Duplicate this page to use with "Trash Town, USA" on page 10. Cut along the dotted lines and give a different "Pollution Problem Card" to each team.

17

Black Death Strikes Europe!

Background:

Around 1350 the bubonic plague, or black death, struck Europe. It began in China, but soon affected most of Europe. Nearly half of Europe's population died as a result of this plague. Many more people died in Asia.

Assignment:

As a young group of scientists, you have been asked to determine the cause of the bubonic plague. Examine the clues provided and construct a theory that explains the cause and spread of this plague.

Procedures:

1. Assign the following roles to each member:
   - clue reader
   - clue organizer
   - recorder
   - spokesperson

2. The clue reader begins by reading each clue to the group.

3. The clue organizer places related clues into groups, as the team begins to sort through the information.

4. As a team, look for cause-and-effect relationships between the clues.

5. As the team reviews the clues, the recorder will note all observations and list any hypotheses that the team develops.

6. After all the clues have been discussed and analyzed, construct your team's theory for the cause of the bubonic plague.

7. Illustrate your team's theory on chart paper. Be sure to include a caption underneath the illustration containing specific details and information about your theory.

8. Help your team's spokesperson prepare a short presentation of your team's theory and illustration for the rest of the class.

©The Education Center, Inc. • *APRIL* • TEC209

Clue Card 1:

Approximately half of Europe's population died from the plague.

Clue Card 6:
Many died within a few days of becoming ill.

Clue Card 2:
An abundance of rats were brought back from Asia on various trade routes.

Clue Card 7:

Business and trade declined during this period of time.

Clue Card 3:

The bacteria is carried throughout the body by the circulatory system.

Clue Card 8:
Cleared land stood unused and idle.

Clue Card 4:
Waste attracts rats. Fleas live on rats.

Clue Card 9:

It was noticed that most people suffering from the plague had flea or rat bites.

Clue Card 5:

Europeans became gravely ill with temperatures of 104°F, vomiting, muscular pain, mental disorganization, and delirium.

Clue Card 10:
People who had the plague suffered from *buboes*—inflamed lymph nodes located throughout the body, especially the inner thigh.

Camouflaged Contaminant

Industry dumps a lot of undesirable chemicals into our water supply. Although rivers have the ability to naturally clean themselves, many chemicals resist being neutralized. Complete the following activity to understand how pollution doesn't have to be visible to be present.

Materials:

• six clear plastic cups

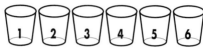

• water

• red food coloring

Red

• one plastic straw

Procedure:

1. Assign each cup a number from 1 to 6. Fill the first cup with water; then add one drop of red food coloring. Stir the mixture using a plastic straw. This represents a harmful chemical. Observe the color of the water.
2. Pour half of the water from the first cup into the second cup. Add fresh water to the second cup until it is full. Observe the color of the water.
3. Pour half of the water from the second cup into the third cup. Add fresh water to the third cup until it is full. Observe the color of the water.
4. Pour half of the water from the third cup into the fourth cup. Add fresh water to the fourth cup until it is full. Observe the color of the water.
5. Repeat the process until you have filled the sixth cup.

Observations:

1. How did the water in each cup change as you added fresh water to it? _____
_____

2. Even though the sixth cup appears to be colorless, does it contain any food coloring? _____
Explain your answer. _____
_____
_____

3. Can a river or lake that looks clean be polluted? _____ Explain your answer. _____
_____
_____

Conclusions: What have you learned about pollution of the earth's water supply? _____
_____
_____

Bonus Box: Can soil that looks clean really be polluted? Explain your answer on the back of this page.

Note to the teacher: Divide the students into groups of three. Make one copy of this page for each group. Give each group the materials listed. Instruct each group to follow the procedures above to complete the experiment. After completing the experiment, have each group state its observations and conclusions to the rest of the class.

Danger Detectives

Thousands of animals are in danger of becoming *extinct,* or dying off, including the blue whale and the giant panda. If any animal, large or small, becomes extinct, it can affect many other animals. For example, if the *krill* (small shrimplike animals) were to become extinct, it would drastically decrease the food supply of whales, seals, fish, and squids. As a result, these animals might become endangered.

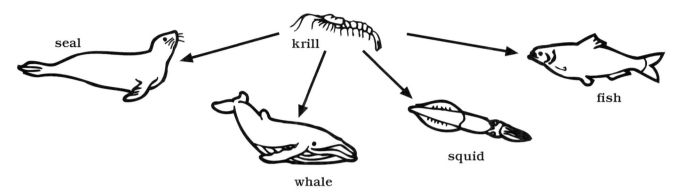

Directions:

As a team, select an endangered animal to research (see the list below for ideas). Find out how this animal is important to humans and/or other animals. Predict what might happen to other animals if it became extinct. Then choose one of the projects below to present your findings to the rest of the class.

Endangered Animals

- Komodo dragon
- snow leopard
- cheetah
- red wolf
- black-footed ferret
- imperial parrot
- green sea turtle
- California condor

Projects:

1. On a piece of poster board, draw a diagram containing several animals that would be affected if the animal you selected became extinct.

2. Write a television commercial to persuade people to help your endangered species. Be sure to include why it is endangered and how its extinction will affect humans.

3. Pretend that you are the selected animal. Write a skit expressing your fears, feelings, and concerns about being endangered.

4. Create a mural of the endangered animal and its habitat. Include information on its name, location, number still in existence, and possible effects to other animals if it becomes extinct.

> **Bonus Box:** On the back of this page, list ways people can help prevent the animal you researched from becoming extinct.

Note to the teacher: Divide the students into groups of three. Duplicate this page for each group. Provide poster board, markers, and other art supplies to groups that need them.

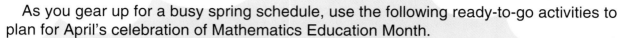

MATH-MONTH MANIA
Activities for Celebrating Mathematics Education Month

As you gear up for a busy spring schedule, use the following ready-to-go activities to plan for April's celebration of Mathematics Education Month.

by Peggy Hambright

Star Wars
Understanding place value, using a calculator

Celebrate Mathematics Education Month with a place-value activity that students will request again and again. Using the digits 1–8 one time each, write any eight-digit number on the board with headings underneath it as shown. Explain to students that the eight digits represent missiles targeted at our spaceship, and that the missiles must be eliminated one at a time in ascending order. Give each student a calculator; then guide him through the directions below. Record the keystrokes that show how to eliminate each digit on the board, and have students copy them.

1. Clear the display.
2. Enter 38,741,526.
3. Identify the place value represented by the digit *1 (thousands place).*
4. Think how this digit's value can be changed to zero *(subtract 1,000).*
5. Press the subtraction key. Enter 1,000. Then press the equal key.
6. Check the display to see whether a zero has replaced the 1 and that the number now reads 38,740,526. If not, reenter the previous display and try again.
7. Subtract 20 to get 38,740,506.
8. Subtract 30,000,000 to get 8,740,506.
9. Subtract 40,000 to get 8,700,506.
10. Subtract 500 to get 8,700,006.
11. Subtract 6 to get 8,700,000.
12. Subtract 700,000 to get 8,000,000.
13. Subtract 8,000,000 to get zero.

For independent practice, give students copies of the top half of page 28 and a different eight-digit number. Have them use the form to record the steps needed to eliminate the assigned number's digits.

38,741,526

Digit	Keystrokes to Eliminate the Digit	Result
1	38,741,526 – 1,000	38,740,526
2	38,740,526 – 20	38,740,506
3	38,740,506 – 30,000,000	8,740,506
4	8,740,506 – 40,000	8,700,506
5	8,700,506 – 500	8,700,006
6	8,700,006 – 6	8,700,000
7	8,700,000 – 700,000	8,000,000
8	8,000,000 – 8,000,000	0

Curved-Angle Designs 🖥

Identifying angles, creating a model with curved-angle designs

Your students' eyes will be following curves with this math-month activity! Challenge students to create curved-angle designs to showcase on a bulletin board. First, help students discover how to construct curved angles. Give each student a copy of the bottom half of page 28 and a ruler. Have students connect the consecutive number pairs in each angle, such as 1 and 2, 3 and 4, and so on.

Next, have students practice *sewing* angles. Give each student a six-inch construction paper square, a large-eyed craft needle, a seven-foot length of solid- or multi-colored cotton Knit-Cro-Sheen® thread, transparent tape, and scissors. Instruct students to follow these directions:

1. Place the acute angle on page 28 on top of the construction paper square. Punch holes with your needle at the numbered marks. Make sure that you make holes in the construction paper.
2. Thread your needle with the seven-foot length of thread. Insert the needle so that it comes up through the paper at 1.
3. Pull the thread through the paper so that just enough of it remains on the back of the paper to tape it down.
4. Continue following the stitching pattern directions on your angle-pattern sheet until all the segments have been sewn.
5. Cut off any extra thread. Tape the end of the thread to the back of the paper.

When students are comfortable with this sewing process, give them larger pieces of construction paper and additional lengths of thread. Ask them to use various sizes of angles to create pictures of sailboats, fishes, or whatever comes to mind! Proudly display students' creations.

CURVED-ANGLE DESIGNS

Geo-Bingo
Reviewing geometry concepts

Radius…trapezoid…in a bingo game? Provide a relaxed setting and resurrect a fashionably old game to review complex geometric terms. Give each student a copy of the patterns on page 29. Have the student cut apart the symbols and randomly glue any 24 of them to his gameboard's spaces. Prepare the game's calling cards by writing each term below on a different index card—laminating these cards if desired. Give each student a small cup of dried beans to use as game markers. Then shuffle the game cards and call them one at a time. Do not precede each call with a bingo letter. Direct students to cover the spaces that match the called clues with their beans. Play until one student wins by filling a row horizontally, vertically, or diagonally. Allow the winner to call the next game.

perpendicular line segments	parallelogram
right angle	rectangle
equilateral triangle	rhombus
scalene triangle	parallel line segments
vertex	quadrilateral
right triangle	octagon
pentagon	circle
square	trapezoid
intersecting line segments	ray
acute angle	closed curve
chord	isosceles triangle
radius	hexagon
line segment	diameter
line	obtuse angle
point	plane

"Tangranimals"
Constructing figures using tangrams, creative writing

Envision a zoo of tangram-shaped animals invading your classroom during Mathematics Education Month. To make this happen, give each student a set of tangram patterns from the top of page 30, an 18" x 24" sheet of colored paper, scissors, glue, and markers. Challenge each student to cut out and then manipulate the tangram's seven pieces to create a real or an imaginary animal on the colored paper. Then have the student glue the tangram pieces on the colored paper. Supply a variety of other art materials so that students can showcase their "tangranimals" in their natural habitats. Display your students' creations on a bulletin board titled "Room [_____]'s Tangram Zoo!" Extend this lesson by having students write adventure stories about their "tangranimals" and share the stories—and their pictures—with younger groups of children.

Math for Young Minds
Reviewing math concepts, creative writing

Are your students capable of communicating math concepts to other youngsters via stories? Why not discover the answer? Gather samples of children's books written to help young minds grasp math concepts (see the list below), and use these books as writing models. Share several of these books aloud with your class to stimulate a brainstorming session about topics for other math-related books. List your students' suggestions on the board. Then challenge each student to choose one of the listed topics or an idea of his own to use to write a story that illustrates a math concept. Further challenge students to transform their edited stories into picture books—with hardback covers if desired. Plan times for your students to share their books with classes of younger students during your math-month celebration.

Alexander, Who Used to Be Rich Last Sunday by Judith Viorst
Anno's Mysterious Multiplying Jar by Mitsumasa Anno
Harriet's Halloween Candy by Nancy Carlson
How Much Is a Million? by David M. Schwartz
If You Made a Million by David M. Schwartz
One Hundred Hungry Ants by Elinor J. Pinczes
A Remainder of One by Elinor J. Pinczes
The Toothpaste Millionaire by Jean Merrill

Measurement Mystery Bags
Measuring using centimeters, graphing and interpreting data

Arouse students' interest in metric measurement during Mathematics Education Month by preparing mystery bags. Fill each bag with three items of varying lengths. Use things that you have on hand, such as lengths of yarn or ribbon, crayons, strips of paper, plastic (or paper) math manipulatives, index cards, markers, and old photographs. Next, cut two ten-unit strips of centimeter-grid paper from page 30 to use as measuring tapes. Place the strips in the bag along with the three objects. Then pair students and give each pair a mystery bag. Instruct each pair to open its bag, measure the lengths of the objects inside with the centimeter strips, and list each item and its measurement on paper. Afterward, have each pair construct a bar graph that shows the differences in the objects' lengths. Then direct each pair to collaborate with another pair of students to write a paragraph that compares their two graphs.

Perceiving Patterns
Identifying and creating continuing patterns

How easy is it to perceive a geometric pattern and continue it? Students will find out with this pattern activity! Make a class supply and a transparency of the centimeter grid on the bottom half of page 30. Color one of the patterns below in the upper left-hand corner of the transparency grid. Then give each student a copy of the grid and crayons or markers. Direct each student to copy onto her grid the pattern shown on the overhead. Have the student continue the pattern to fill her grid. If desired, challenge students to duplicate and extend one of the remaining patterns.

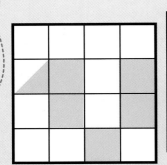 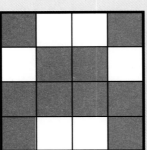 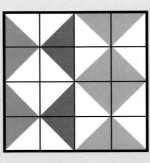 

Gridiron Competition
Identifying coordinate pairs, problem solving

Your math-month celebration has never known team competition like this! Prepare a gameboard by copying the grid below on poster board, laminating it for use with a wipe-off marker. Display the resulting grid with a cutout of an obstacle, such as a hurdle or a bridge, pinned to it at (4, 4).

Next, divide your class into two teams. Explain that the object of the game is to be the first team to reach the finish line. Further explain that each team must draw a continuous line stretching from its starting point either across or up the grid to the obstacle, and from there to the finish line opposite its team name. Begin play by having a child from Team A call out a set of coordinates for plotting its starting point (0, –). Allow a child from Team B to do the same (–, 0). Plot these points that identify the starting points for both teams with different-colored wipe-off markers. Before having the second player on each team call out the next coordinate pair, explain that from now on the lines can advance only one square at a time. Remind players that they should choose their coordinates carefully so that the lines lead toward the obstacle first and then to the finish line.

Increase the difficulty level of subsequent rounds by adding a new obstacle to the gameboard each time—and requiring each one to be reached in sequence!

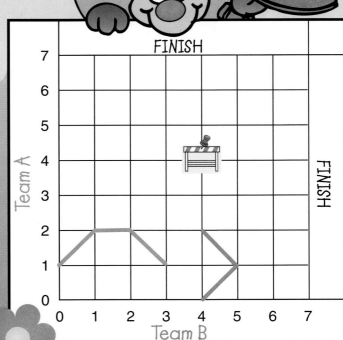

26

Chances Are...
Making and testing probability predictions

Include several probability explorations in your Mathematics Education Month celebration. Set up a probability center in your classroom where students will conduct a series of investigations. First, duplicate each activity below. Next, bag the materials needed for Activities 2 and 3 and then attach each activity's directions to the outside of its bag. Place Activity 1 and the bags at the center along with paper and pencils. As students visit the center, instruct them to copy the chart from each sheet onto paper before starting the activity. Remind students to record their tallies for each activity in the chart.

Activity 1: Predict how many times a 3 will be rolled if you roll a die 30 times. Record your prediction on your paper. Then roll the die 30 times. Tally each result in your chart. How close was your prediction to the actual outcome?

My prediction: _____

Outcome	Tally
Rolled a 3	
Did Not Roll a 3	

Activity 2: Inside this bag are one yellow card and two green cards. Without looking, draw two cards from the bag. Are these two cards the same color or are they different? Record your answer with a tally mark. Replace the cards in the bag. Then draw out two cards 29 more times—each time recording the result with a tally mark. When you have finished drawing 30 times and tallying, circle the outcome that occurred more often.

Outcome	Tally
Same Color	
Different Colors	

Activity 3: Toss the penny that's inside this bag. Record how it lands. Repeat the toss nine more times, recording each tally mark in the column for 1st Tally. Did heads or tails turn up more often? Do you think the outcome will be different if you repeat the test? Toss the penny another ten times and record the tally marks in the column for 2nd Tally. Compare the outcomes of the two tests.

Outcome	1st Tally	2nd Tally
Heads		
Tails		

Star Wars

Enter the eight-digit number your teacher gives you in the box below.
Then write the steps to show how to eliminate it.

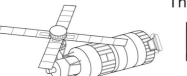

Digit	Keystrokes to Eliminate the Digit	Resulting Number in Display
1	_____	_____
2	_____	_____
3	_____	_____
4	_____	_____
5	_____	_____
6	_____	_____
7	_____	_____
8	_____	_____

Note to the teacher: Make one copy of this form for each student to use with "Star Wars" on page 22.

Patterns

Use with "Curved-Angle Designs" on page 23.

Stitching pattern directions:
Stitch up through 1, down through 2; up through 3, down through 4; etc.

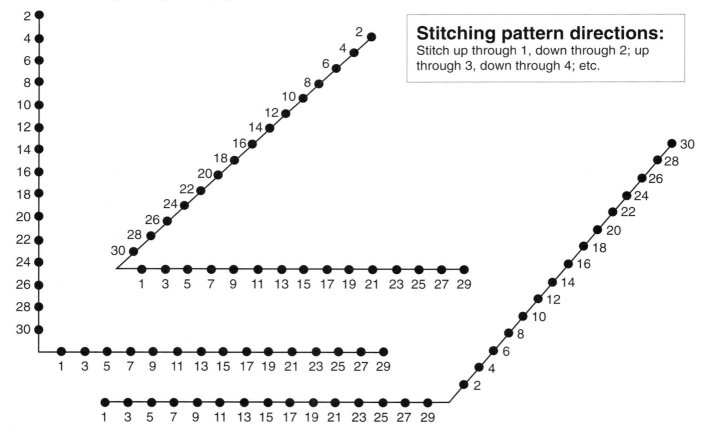

GEO-
BINGO

FREE

Tangram Patterns

Use with " 'Tangranimals' " on page 24.

Centimeter Grid

Use with "Measurement Mystery Bags" on page 25 and "Perceiving Patterns" on page 26.

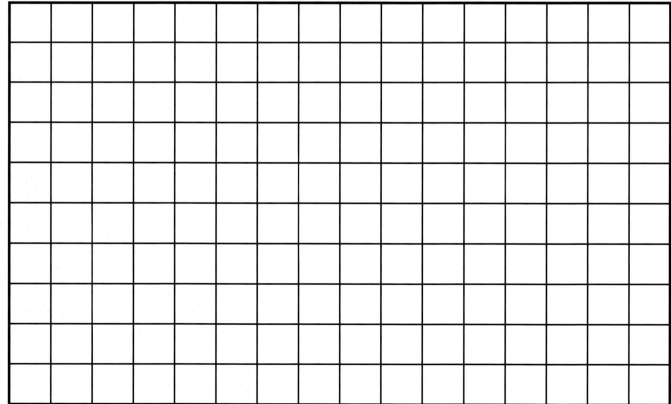

Riddles in Reverse

Professor Backwards works in a topsy-turvy fashion. He likes to give the answers and then ask the riddles! Find the answers he has supplied by combining the fractional parts of the word clues. Then help him write an appropriate question for each answer.

Example: 1/2 of polish + 1/4 of yard + 3/4 of gone = **polygon**
What is a simple, closed figure that has line segments as sides?
or
What did the pirate say when he realized his parrot was gone?

1. 4/6 of decide + 3/4 of malt = _____
    4/4 of numb + 2/5 of erase = _____
    _____ ?

2. 2/9 of different + 2/5 of visit + 3/6 of denote + 1/4 of dive = _____
    _____ ?

3. 2/9 of president + 2/9 of immediate + 1/5 of eagle = _____
    1/3 of new + 3/8 of umbrella + 2/5 of error = _____
    _____ ?

4. 2/3 of period + 1/3 of man + 1/2 of eternity = _____
    _____ ?

5. 3/5 of squid + 3/4 of area = _____
    _____ ?

6. 1/2 of symbol + 2/2 of me + 4/5 of trick = _____
    _____ ?

7. 3/4 of face + 2/7 of tonight + 1/5 of right = _____
    _____ ?

8. 1/3 of grapes + 1/5 of apple + 1/5 of photograph = _____
    _____ ?

9. 3/8 of consider + 2/5 of grade + 1/4 of ugly + 3/5 of enter = _____
    1/3 of answer + 1/3 of glance + 1/3 of escape = _____
    _____
    _____ ?

10. 1/8 of remember + 3/7 of homonym
    + 3/3 of bus = _____
    _____
    _____ ?

Bonus Box: Why is 8, 5, 4, 9, 1, 7, 6, 3, 2, 0 a logical arrangement of the numerals 0 to 9?

What a Workout!

Complete the following workout to keep your problem-solving strategies in good condition! Show your work in the spaces provided.

1. Alan wants to work up to doing 50 sit-ups a day. He plans to start with 20 and add 3 more each day. On which day will Alan do 50 sit-ups? Fill in the chart to show your answer.

Day	1	2	3														
Number of Sit-Ups	20																

2. Alan went shopping for new workout clothes. He purchased three T-shirts: blue, red, and white. He bought three pairs of mesh shorts: black, gray, and brown. He also got three towels: striped, solid-colored, and checked. How many combinations can Alan make? Extend and label the tree diagram to show all of the possible combinations for Alan on the back of this sheet.

3. Alan's two friends, Jeremy and Trevor, asked to meet him at the Y to work out. One boy had his mother bring him by car, one walked, and the other rode his bicycle. Jeremy did not walk. Alan did not come by car. Trevor rode his bike. How did Alan get to the Y? Complete the chart by marking a √ in a box for a match and an X if no match is possible.

	Alan	Jeremy	Trevor
Traveled by Car			
Walked			
Rode a Bicycle			

4. Alan decided to add bicycling to his workout schedule. The shop he visited carried bicycles and tricycles. If there were 48 wheels and 18 cycles in all, how many bicycles were in the shop? Continue the chart to find out.

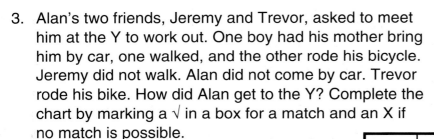

Number of Tricycles	Number of Tricycle Wheels	Number of Bicycles	Number of Bicycle Wheels	Total Number of Cycles	Total Number of Wheels
1	3	17	34	18	37
2	6	16	32	18	38
3	9	15	30	18	39

Talking Calculators

Has your calculator ever "talked" to you? Use your calculator to work each problem below. After working each problem, turn your calculator upside down to read a word that completes the sentence.

Example: 1692 x 2 + 4331 = **7715 = sill.** Jill sat on the window **sill.**

1. 2 x 3 ÷ 10 = _____ = _____
   Jay plans to _____ skating on Saturday afternoon.

2. 24234 ÷ 3 = _____ = _____
   Kate dropped a _____ of glue on her art paper.

3. 82 + 428 + 96 + 31 − 19 = _____ = _____
   The Coxes were making _____ plans for their vacation.

4. 5721.4 + 2016.6 = _____ = _____
   School was dismissed at the sound of the _____.

5. 894 − 215 − 72 = _____ = _____
   The heavy _____ floated easily down the river.

6. (1640 x 3) + (1397 x 2) = _____ = _____
   The caravan came into town after rounding a _____.

7. 1816.4 + 1690.6 = _____ = _____
   Courtney and Jan had not meant to _____ their way.

8. 56358 − 8641 − 2055 − 5520 − 2066 = _____ = _____
   Use the _____ to locate the Pacific and Indian oceans.

9. A. 4896 + 2209 = _____ = _____
   B. 46296 ÷ 6 = _____ = _____
   The fish lay on the _____ with the hook caught in its _____.
   (A)   (B)

10. A. 89 x 15 x 5 + 1043 = _____ = _____
    B. 312 x 5 x 2 − 75 = _____ = _____
    The _____ for repairing the _____ was $5.75.
    (A)   (B)

Bonus Box: Write a talking-calculator problem on the back of this sheet for a friend to solve. Use this key: 0 = O, 1 = I, 2 = Z, 3 = E, 4 = H, 5 = S, 6 = G, 7 = L, 8 = B.

Keep 'em Laughin'

A good dose of humor in a lesson can cure the "learning blues" that sometimes sweep through a classroom! What better time than April—National Humor Month—to rid your classroom of those blues? The following activities are sure to tickle your students' funny bones while giving their brains a workout. (And who said learning can't be fun!)

by Simone Lepine and Thad McLaurin

Tickle Your Funny Bone
Motivating students

Tickle your funny bone with this bulletin board idea! Cover a bulletin board with bright paper; then title it "Tickle Your Funny Bone." Divide your students into five groups to create a "class clown" similar to the one shown below. Assign each group one of the following sections: feet, legs and waist, torso and arms, head, or hat. Provide each group with a variety of colored paper, markers, glue, scissors, and glitter. (Give each group specific dimensions to ensure a good fit between sections.) After each group has completed its section, tack the sections together on the bulletin board. For fun, have the class select a humorous name for the class clown.

To complete the board, make enough copies of page 43 to give each student at least one bone pattern. Explain that each student is to write a funny joke on his bone. Give students a couple of days to find jokes or create original ones; then collect the bones and display them on the board as shown. To make the display more colorful and fun, purchase some craft feathers and staple them around the bones. Encourage students to read the jokes during free time.

Laughter Is the Best Medicine
Making a personal connection

What makes your students laugh? Give each student the opportunity to find out what makes his classmates laugh with the following activity. Gather a class supply of craft sticks. Divide the sticks into pairs. Using a permanent marker, label each pair with a different number; then give each student one stick. Have each student search for his classmate with the matching number. Instruct the student to spend one minute expressing something that makes him laugh. Then have the student exchange craft sticks with a different student. Repeat the process until each student has shared what makes him laugh with four or five students. After completing the activity, have students discuss the different responses. List them on a large piece of chart paper to hang in the classroom.

I like elephant jokes.

Reading *Garfield* makes me laugh.

A pie in the face gets me every time!

The Three Stooges makes me laugh.

Home-video bloopers are hilarious!

Knock, Knock!

Who's there?

Knock, Knock! Who's There?
Writing for a purpose

Sure, knock-knock jokes are pretty corny, but kids love them! Supply your classroom with knock-knock joke books from the library. Also, ask students to bring joke books from home. Tell each student to select one knock-knock joke from the supply of joke books or to create an original one. Duplicate the door pattern (page 44) on colored paper for each student. Then instruct each student to cut out his door pattern and place it on a sheet of notebook paper. Have each student trace around the door onto the notebook paper; then cut out the tracing. The beginning of the joke ("Knock! Knock! Who's there?") is already printed on the front of each student's door. Instruct the student to finish the joke by writing the one he's selected on the piece of notebook paper. Then have each student place the door pattern on top of the notebook paper and staple the left-hand side to create a booklet. Display the booklets by stapling or taping just the notebook-paper page to a bulletin board or wall.

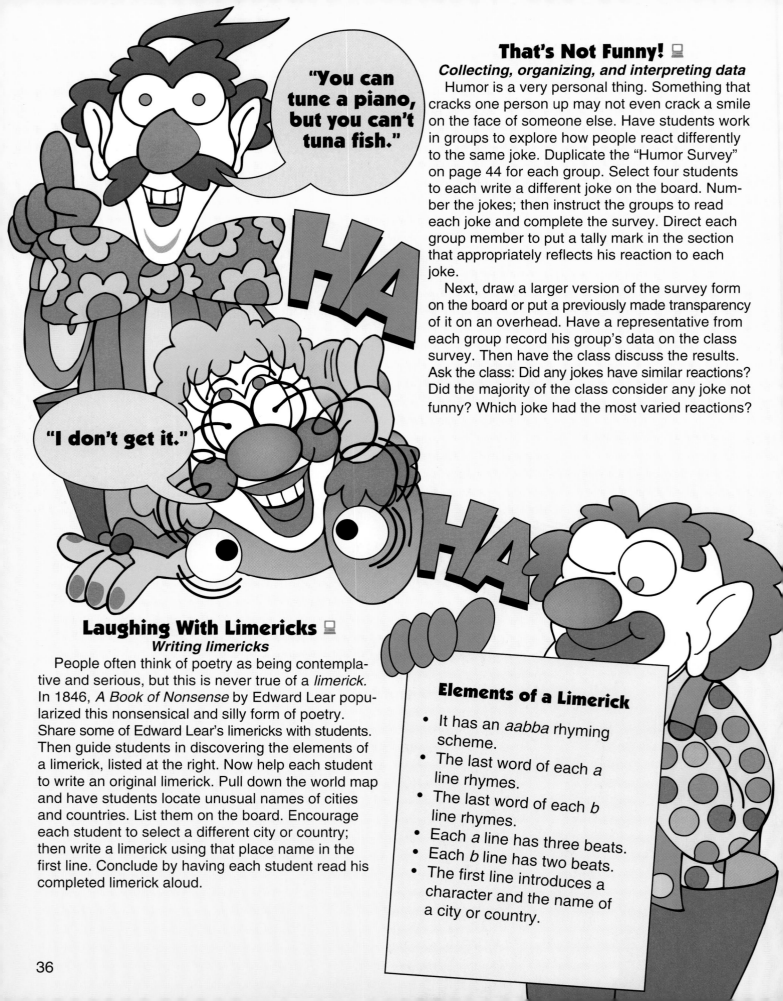

"You can tune a piano, but you can't tuna fish."

"I don't get it."

HA HA HA

That's Not Funny!
Collecting, organizing, and interpreting data

Humor is a very personal thing. Something that cracks one person up may not even crack a smile on the face of someone else. Have students work in groups to explore how people react differently to the same joke. Duplicate the "Humor Survey" on page 44 for each group. Select four students to each write a different joke on the board. Number the jokes; then instruct the groups to read each joke and complete the survey. Direct each group member to put a tally mark in the section that appropriately reflects his reaction to each joke.

Next, draw a larger version of the survey form on the board or put a previously made transparency of it on an overhead. Have a representative from each group record his group's data on the class survey. Then have the class discuss the results. Ask the class: Did any jokes have similar reactions? Did the majority of the class consider any joke not funny? Which joke had the most varied reactions?

Laughing With Limericks
Writing limericks

People often think of poetry as being contemplative and serious, but this is never true of a *limerick.* In 1846, *A Book of Nonsense* by Edward Lear popularized this nonsensical and silly form of poetry. Share some of Edward Lear's limericks with students. Then guide students in discovering the elements of a limerick, listed at the right. Now help each student to write an original limerick. Pull down the world map and have students locate unusual names of cities and countries. List them on the board. Encourage each student to select a different city or country; then write a limerick using that place name in the first line. Conclude by having each student read his completed limerick aloud.

Elements of a Limerick

- It has an *aabba* rhyming scheme.
- The last word of each *a* line rhymes.
- The last word of each *b* line rhymes.
- Each *a* line has three beats.
- Each *b* line has two beats.
- The first line introduces a character and the name of a city or country.

The "Ha-Ha" Game
Motivating students
Challenge your students' self-control with the Ha-Ha Game. Have your class sit in a circle. Pick one person to begin the game by saying, "Ha." The person to her left then says, "Ha-ha." Each person adds one more "Ha" as the game continues around the circle. The object of the game is to see how far the game can continue until someone breaks out into natural laughter while doing her forced "Ha, ha's." It's harder than you think!

A "Punny" Activity
Understanding puns, writing for a purpose
"My English teacher is like a judge. She's always handing out sentences!" Jokes like this one containing a *pun*—a play on words—have been around for a long time. They challenge the mind and make you laugh at the same time. The humor comes from the play on words in which one word has two meanings. Puns can also be presented as riddles, such as "What did the bull with no money do at the shopping mall? Charge!" See how many words your students can think of that have more than one meaning. Duplicate " 'Punny' Words" on page 45 for each student. Have each student copy any words from the class list that do not appear on the reproducible. Finally, instruct each student to create original jokes or riddles using as many words from page 45 as possible. Then hold a "Pun Time" and have each student read at least one of her jokes or riddles to the rest of the class.

Stop Pulling My Leg
Understanding and interpreting idioms

If taken literally, *idioms* (language or expressions unique to a people) can be quite humorous. Duplicate "Pardon the Expression" on page 45 for each student. Also give each student one sheet of drawing paper and crayons or markers. Have each student choose an idiom on page 45 and illustrate the literal meaning of it. Tell the student to make his drawing humorous and as literal as possible, but not to "let the cat out of the bag." Have each student present his drawing to the rest of the class. Call on students to try to guess which idiom the student has illustrated. Post the drawings in the hallway for other students to enjoy.

Stop pulling my leg!

Pam Crane

I'm going to blow my stack!

HA HA HA HA HA

"Mime" Your Own Business
Understanding and interpreting idioms

What's the matter? Cat got your tongue? Well, that's perfect for this game because no talking is allowed. Divide students into groups of two or three; then give each group a different idiom from "Pardon the Expression" on page 45. Instruct each group to create a mime presentation revealing the literal meaning of its idiom for the rest of the class. Make sure each group keeps its idiom a secret while rehearsing its presentation. The students will have more fun than a barrel of monkeys trying to guess each group's idiom!

Trip the Tongue and Triple the Fun!
Understanding alliteration, writing for a purpose

A tongue twister may not be saying anything particularly humorous, but when you try to say one or hear someone else try to say one, it becomes very humorous. The faster you say it, the funnier it becomes. Tongue twisters make use of *alliteration*—the repetition of one initial sound several times in a phrase—to trip the tongue.

Check to see if your library has a copy of *Fox in Socks* by Dr. Seuss. This book creates wonderful tongue-twisting tales for children. Also check out *Six Sick Sheep* by Joanna Cole. It contains a wonderful collection of twisters.

Ask students to share some of their favorite tongue twisters. Then have each student learn more about alliteration and experiment with writing an original tongue twister by completing the reproducible on page 46. Conclude your study of tongue twisters with the following two games:

• **The Fastest Mouth in the West:** For this game find a stopwatch and several long tongue twisters, such as "Peter Piper." Have each student repeat the tongue twister as fast as he can without making any mistakes. Specify that each word must be articulated clearly. Use the stopwatch to time each student. Treat the student with the fastest and most understandable mouth with a special prize. Repeat the game with several tongue twisters to give more students a crack at winning. (A previous winner doesn't participate in subsequent tongue twisters.) In case disagreements occur, tape-record each student for an instant replay.

• **More Is Better:** Materials for this game include a stopwatch and several short tongue twisters, such as "She sells seashells by the seashore," "Red leather, yellow leather," "Double bubble gum bubbles double," or "Rubber baby buggy bumpers." This game determines who in your classroom can correctly repeat a tongue twister the most times in one minute. Time each student. If a student "trips" over his tongue, he's out! Repeat the game with several tongue twisters over several days to give more students a chance of winning. (A previous winner doesn't participate in subsequent tongue twisters.)

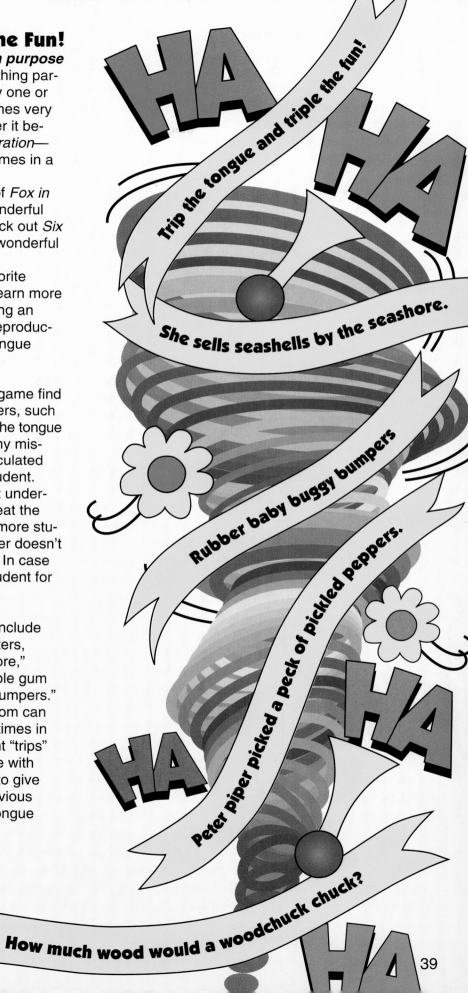

Are Comics Just for Kids?
Collecting, organizing, and interpreting data

Both children and adults enjoy reading comic strips. The type of humor varies with each comic strip. Have your students list some of the popular comic strips of today. Then ask each student to tell which cartoon listed he finds the most humorous and why. After each student has shared his opinion, point out that not everyone has the same taste in comics. Next, take a class poll to find if there are one or two comic strips listed that most of the students enjoy reading. Then have students give examples of comics they think appeal more to adults. To see if they are correct, have the students poll their parents to find out their favorite comic strips. Tally the results on the board the next day; then have students discuss possible reasons for the outcome.

As an extension activity, invite the editor of your local newspaper's comic page to come and speak about the process of putting the comic section together. Also ask the editor to make available the addresses and email accounts of students' favorite cartoonists.

Ka-pow! Zap! Boom! Whoosh!
Understanding teamwork, working cooperatively

Comic book series first appeared in the 1930s and have been popular ever since. There are many people involved in making a comic book. First, a *writer* creates stories that can be easily illustrated. Then an *editor* decides which stories are used in the comic books. Next, a *penciller* draws each scene; then an *inker* goes over the penciller's art with permanent ink. A *letterer* hand-prints each dialogue caption for every scene. Finally, a *colorist* adds color to the inked drawings.

Have students experience the process of creating a comic book page with the following activity. Divide students into groups of four. Duplicate page 47 for each group. Then have each group select a penciller, inker, letterer, and colorist. Instruct group members to work together to write and edit their page. Next, have group members complete their assigned jobs in the appropriate order. Schedule a time for each group to present its page to the rest of the class. Conclude by having students discuss the pros and cons of the process. Encourage each group to continue working on its comic book during free time.

Where's the Punch Line?
Drawing conclusions

Many comic strips reveal the punch line to the reader in the last scene. In the following activity, the punch line is missing. Several weeks ahead of time, start collecting comic strips that give the punch lines in the last scenes. When you've collected four or five, make a photocopy of each; then white-out the dialogue in the last scene of each original comic strip. Mount each original strip to a separate sheet of construction paper; then post each strip around the classroom. Also tape an envelope to the bottom of each sheet of construction paper. Instruct each student to try to guess the punch line of each comic strip over the next few days. Tell the student to record each guess on a small slip of paper with his name and place it in the appropriate envelope. At the end of the week, read the responses for each comic strip. Give prizes to the students who guess correctly. Also give prizes to any students who develop better punch lines than the originals.

For an added challenge, white-out the dialogue of an entire strip and see if the students can figure out the joke and punch line from just the drawings.

Joking Around
Responding to literature

Have you ever been the victim of a practical joke? Practical jokes can be very funny, but sometimes they can turn sour. *The War With Grandpa* by Robert K. Smith explores this type of humor. The main character of the story, Peter, finds himself booted out of his room when his grandfather moves in with the family. Peter declares war on his grandfather with a series of practical joke attacks. The grandfather responds with a few practical jokes of his own. The war is fun for a while until the practical jokes turn mean-spirited and the consequences are no longer funny. Peter and his grandfather learn that war is not the answer. Read aloud *The War With Grandpa* to your class. Have students discuss problems that can occur with practical jokes. Also discuss how Peter and his grandfather eventually solve their problems.

Reading Is Fun(ny)
Responding to literature, participating in an oral presentation

Everyone loves to read a funny book! Children's literature contains a never-ending supply of books that make children laugh. Have the librarian find a collection of humorous stories and poems to read to your class. Then have students share the names of books that they found humorous. List the titles on the board. Once the list is complete, group the students according to the books they found humorous. Instruct each group to create a presentation that will express the humor of the book. The following is a list of suggested ways each group can present the humorous aspects of its book:

- Reenact a funny scene in the book.
- Make a television commercial pitching the book.
- Create a mock interview and ask the author or characters in the book questions about a humorous event.
- Illustrate a humorous scene from the book.
- Read a humorous scene from the book to motivate others to check out the book.

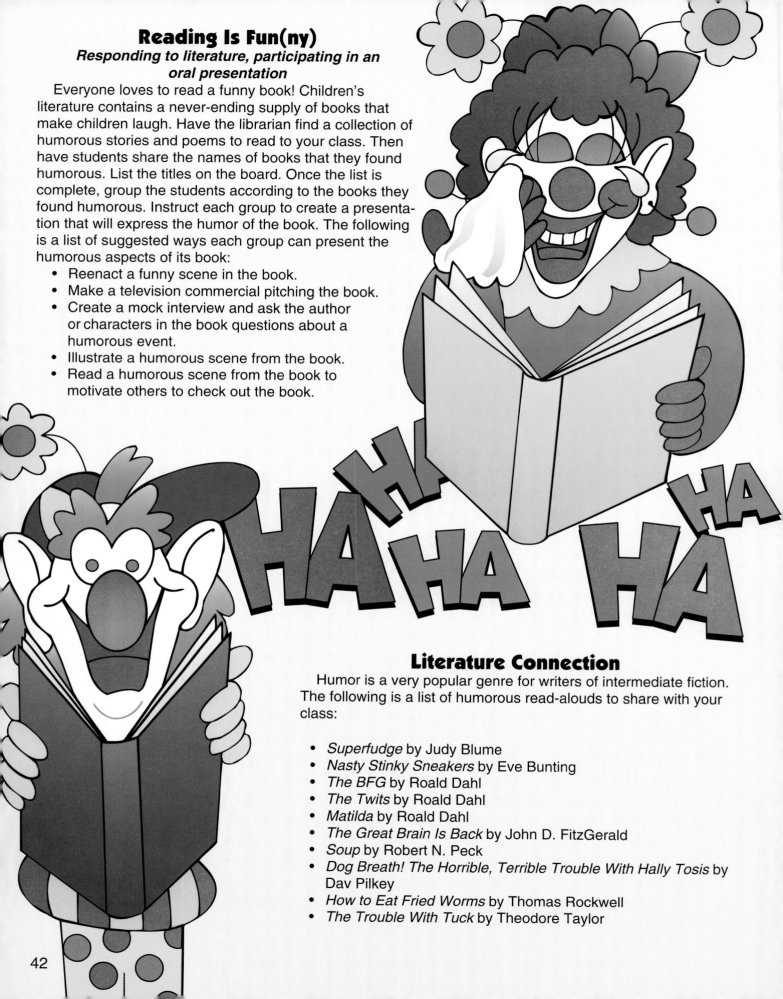

Literature Connection
Humor is a very popular genre for writers of intermediate fiction. The following is a list of humorous read-alouds to share with your class:

- *Superfudge* by Judy Blume
- *Nasty Stinky Sneakers* by Eve Bunting
- *The BFG* by Roald Dahl
- *The Twits* by Roald Dahl
- *Matilda* by Roald Dahl
- *The Great Brain Is Back* by John D. FitzGerald
- *Soup* by Robert N. Peck
- *Dog Breath! The Horrible, Terrible Trouble With Hally Tosis* by Dav Pilkey
- *How to Eat Fried Worms* by Thomas Rockwell
- *The Trouble With Tuck* by Theodore Taylor

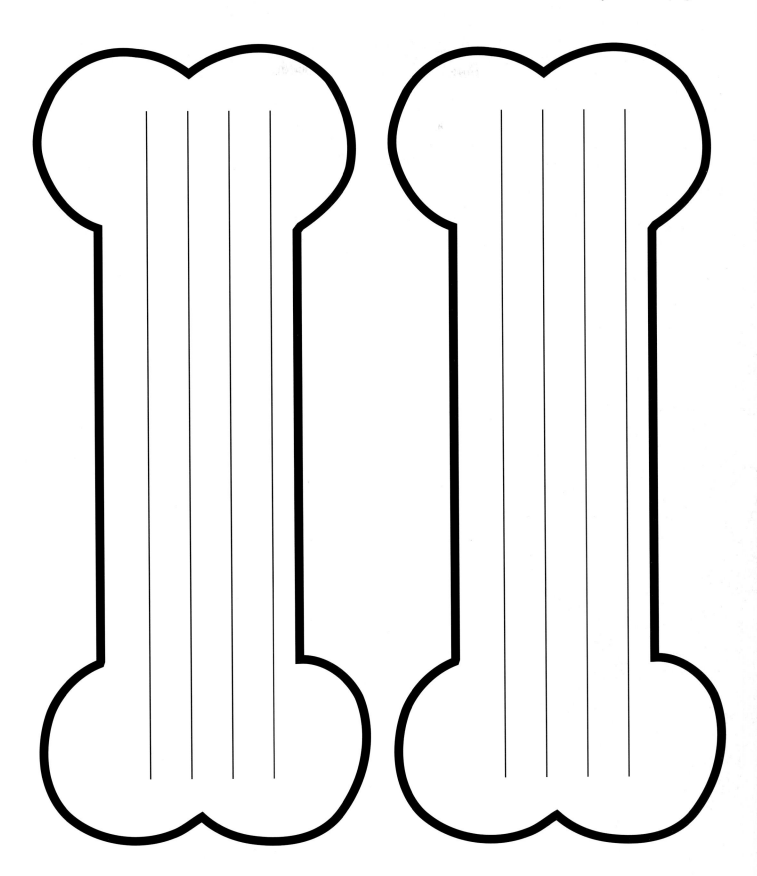

Pattern
Use with "Knock, Knock! Who's There?" on page 35.

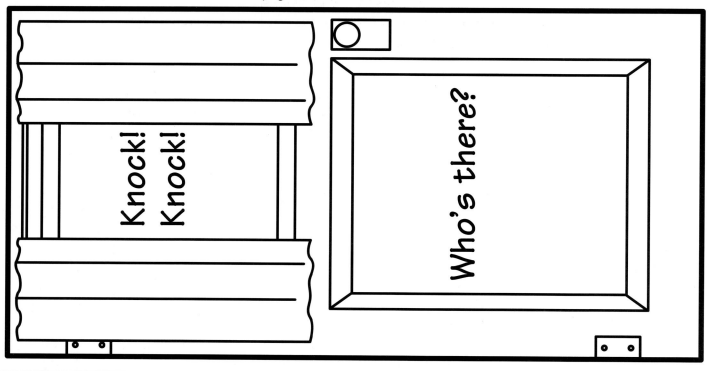

Group Members _____ *Taking a survey*

Humor Survey

	Laugh Out Loud	Snicker	Smile	Not Funny
Joke #1				
Joke #2				
Joke #3				
Joke #4				

©The Education Center, Inc. • *APRIL* • TEC209

Note to the teacher: Make one copy of the "Humor Survey" for each group. Use the survey with "That's Not Funny!" on page 36.

"Punny" Words

Homophones and words with multiple meanings make great puns. Use the list of words below to create your own "punny" jokes and riddles.

- bank
- bark
- batter
- bill
- bright
- charge
- dry
- fan
- foot
- left
- mammoth
- racket
- sentence
- shed
- spring
- star
- suspended
- watch

- hoarse
- horse
- heard
- herd
- hour
- our
- die
- dye
- waist
- waste
- whale
- wail
- Rome
- roam
- reel
- real
- peace
- piece

- knead
- need
- flea
- flee
- Greece
- grease
- sail
- sale
- pole
- poll
- doe
- dough
- miner
- minor
- knight
- night
- dessert
- desert

- hire
- higher
- weak
- week
- toe
- tow

What do you call running through the desert?

A dry run.

©The Education Center, Inc. • *APRIL* • TEC209

Pardon the Expression

Listed below are 20 common English expressions, or *idioms.* Pick one; then create a humorous illustration of its literal meaning.

1. He bawled his eyes out.
2. Go fly a kite.
3. She's on top of the world.
4. I'm fit as a fiddle.
5. He's in a pickle.
6. Hold your horses!
7. He's as ill as a hornet.
8. There's a fork in the road.
9. She had to blow off some steam.
10. He's skating on thin ice.

Have you ever been tongue-tied?

11. He has a frog in his throat.
12. Take the bull by the horns.
13. I have a bone to pick with you.
14. He must have rocks in his head.
15. Mom has a splitting headache.
16. You are driving me up the wall!
17. Dad will keep an eye on the baby.
18. The judge will throw the book at her.
19. She'd be tickled pink to see you again.
20. Money always burns a hole in her pocket.

Have your eyes ever been bigger than your stomach?

©The Education Center, Inc. • *APRIL* • TEC209

Note to the teacher: Duplicate " 'Punny' Words" for each student and use with "A 'Punny' Activity" on page 37. Duplicate "Pardon the Expression" for each student and use with "Stop Pulling My Leg" and " 'Mime' Your Own Business" on page 38.

Trip the Tongue and Triple the Fun

A tongue twister may not be saying anything particularly humorous, but when you try to say one or hear someone else try to say one, it becomes very funny. The faster you say it, the funnier it becomes. Some tongue twisters use *alliteration* to trip the tongue. Alliteration is the repetition of one initial sound in several words within a sentence.

Tongue twisters such as "Peter Piper picked a peck of pickled peppers" and "How much wood would a woodchuck chuck" are long and fun to say. In the space below, create your own long tongue twister. Pick one main initial sound to repeat as much as possible in your twister and remember to make it humorous.

_____ (Title) _____ _____ _____ _____ _____ _____	Illustrate your tongue twister in the space below.

Other tongue twisters, such as "She sells seashells by the seashore" and "Red leather, yellow leather," are short but are very hard to repeat quickly several times in a row. In the space below, create your own short tongue twister. See how many of your classmates can quickly repeat your twister five times.

_____

_____

TONGUE TWISTERS

Note to the teacher: Duplicate this page for each student to use with "Trip the Tongue and Triple the Fun!" on page 39.

Working cooperatively

THE COMIC BOOK

Use the space below to create the first page of your group's comic book. As a whole group, brainstorm story ideas that can be easily illustrated. Select one idea; then write the dialogue for each scene on a separate sheet of paper. Next, the *penciller, inker, letterer,* and *colorist* complete their assigned jobs.

Note to the teacher: Duplicate this page for each student to use with "Ka-pow! Zap! Boom! Whoosh!" on page 40.

AMAZING OCEANS

Looking down from space, the oceans appear to cover the entire planet—earning Earth its nickname, the "Blue Planet." What kind of environment is this vast expanse of clear blue water? What mysteries lie beneath its surface? Introduce your students to the amazing world of our oceans with the following thematic activities, reproducibles, and literature suggestions.

by Irene Taylor, Pat Wimberley, and Thad McLaurin

THE OCEAN—A COMPLEX ECOSYSTEM
Building background information

The oceans cover 71 percent of the earth's surface. The Atlantic, Pacific, Indian, and Arctic oceans make up the four large bodies of water separating the continents. The many seas, bays, and gulfs are actually smaller parts of these four oceans.

An ocean is a complex *ecosystem* containing a vast number of unusual creatures and plants that are specially adapted to live in their salty world. Each ocean layer, or *zone,* holds its own unique sea life. From the countless plankton that provide the basis for the food chain to the luminescent creatures that live in the very deepest, darkest, and coldest regions—all are joined together in a complex web of life. As the modern world impacts the oceans through pollution and misuse, it often threatens the sea life that inhabits each ocean layer.

Many mysterious secrets of the ocean have been unlocked through modern-day exploration. We now know of the ocean's rugged floor, with areas deeper than the highest mountains found on land. We've learned about the amazing creatures that can exist at great depths—withstanding cold, darkness, and great pressures. We've discovered the many riches the ocean provides, such as food, minerals, medicines, and energy sources.

Many questions still remain unanswered. Finding the answers to these questions is becoming more and more important as human dependence on the ocean grows.

3-D Ocean

Researching ocean organisms, creating a model

Breathe life into your ocean studies with the following three-dimensional bulletin board activity. Inform students that ocean life is divided into three groups: *plankton, nekton,* and *benthos. Plankton* include plantlike organisms and animals, such as diatoms and jellyfish, that drift in the upper layers of the ocean. *Nekton* are made up of free-swimming animals, such as fish, that live in surface and deep waters. *Benthos* consist of plants and animals, such as kelp and starfish, that live on the ocean floor.

Have students work in six research teams. Assign two teams to research each of the three ocean-life groups. Instruct each team to find information on the feeding habits and the physical traits of two organisms from its group. Make sure each group selects different organisms. Instruct each group to follow the directions below to create a model of each organism.

Cover a large bulletin board with blue paper. Along the bottom of the board, tack a thin strip of brown paper to represent the ocean floor. Label the name of each ocean-life group on a separate 2" x 11" strip of white paper; then post the strips on the board as shown. Hang an old soccer net from the ceiling and drape it across the bulletin board. Attach each model to the board or place it in the net. Add other sea-related items such as a lobster trap, shells, or driftwood. After all the models are displayed, have each team give a short presentation identifying and describing its models.

Materials for each group:
4 large sheets of butcher paper, tissue paper, scissors, glue, paint, paintbrushes, markers

Directions:
1. Place two sheets of butcher paper on top of each other. Draw the shape of one organism on the top sheet. Be as accurate as you can with size and shape.
2. Cut out the drawing, making sure to cut through both sheets of paper.
3. Paint both sides of the model as accurately as you can. Add details using markers.
4. Glue the outer edges of the drawing together, leaving an opening at the top.
5. Stuff the model with tissue paper; then glue the opening together.
6. Repeat the first five steps to create the second model.

THE BLUE PLANET
Understanding the structure of the earth's surface, making a visual presentation

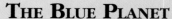

Earth differs from all the other planets in our solar system. It has liquid water. Because there is water, there is life. Help students understand the impact water has on Earth by having them examine a globe. Hold the globe up in front of your students. Ask them if there is more land or more water represented on the globe. Next, point out how the four oceans are interconnected. Tell the students that Earth is often called the "Blue Planet." Ask why Earth might be given this nickname. *(The vast amount of water covering Earth makes the planet appear mostly blue in pictures taken from outer space.)* Inform your students that water covers more than 70 percent of Earth's surface. To help students visualize 70 percent, give each student a piece of graph paper containing 100 squares. (Half-inch graph paper works well for this activity.) Instruct each student to randomly color 30 squares green and 70 squares blue. Then tell students that the green squares represent the amount of land on Earth, and the blue squares represent the amount of water covering Earth's surface. Conclude the activity by having students brainstorm other nicknames for Earth.

LITERATURE CONNECTION
Dive into your ocean unit with the following literature suggestions:

- *The Eyes of the Amaryllis* by Natalie Babbitt
- *Call It Courage* by Armstrong Sperry
- *The Black Pearl* by Scott O'Dell
- *Loch* by Paul Zindel
- *Strange Eating Habits of Sea Creatures* by Jean Sibbald
- *Mysteries of the Ocean Deep* by Dr. Frances Dipper

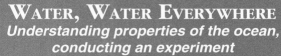

WATER, WATER EVERYWHERE
Understanding properties of the ocean, conducting an experiment

Although most of Earth's surface is covered with water, only a small amount is suitable for use by land organisms—85 percent of all water on Earth is seawater. Seawater contains 11 main chemical components and nearly every known natural element. One of the most abundant chemical components in seawater is salt. An average gallon of seawater contains six ounces of salt. This salt comes from several sources, including the weathering of rocks on land and volcanic activity on land and under water.

With such an abundance of water in the world, why can't we use this salt water to irrigate farmland during periods of drought? Give your students an opportunity to study the effects of salt water on plants by having them work in small groups to conduct the experiment on page 56. Duplicate page 56 for each group. Then supply each group with the materials listed on the reproducible. After conducting the experiment for 14 days, have each group present its findings. Discuss possible reasons for the outcomes.

Freshwater

Salt water

IN MINUTE DETAIL
Descriptive writing

Sharpen your students' descriptive-writing skills with the following activity. Ask each student to bring in one seashell. Gather some extra shells for students who do not have one. Give each student five minutes to examine her shell and brainstorm a list of words and phrases that describe her shell's unique features. Make a class supply of the shell pattern on page 57. Challenge each student to use her list of words and phrases to write a descriptive paragraph, riddle, or poem on the lined pattern. Instruct her to leave her name off the pattern.

Create the following interactive bulletin board to display the descriptions and shells. Have each student cut out her shell pattern. Then assign each student a number to write on the back of the pattern. Display each shell pattern on a bulletin board titled "Treasures of the Deep." Staple each pattern at the top so that the number can be seen by lifting the bottom. Place the shells on a table under the bulletin board. Write the corresponding number for each shell on a small piece of tape and stick it under the appropriate shell. During free time, direct each student to visit the display, read a description on the board, and then select a shell from the table that she thinks matches the description she just read. Have her check the accuracy of her guess by looking to see if the two numbers match.

OCEAN LAYER FLIP BOOKS 💻
Understanding properties of the ocean, researching ocean zones

Descend into the ocean depths and you will pass through four distinct layers on your way to the ocean floor. The deeper you go, the colder and darker the water becomes.

The most productive layer—the *sunlight zone*—lies just beneath the surface of the ocean and extends down to 650 feet. Beneath the sunlight zone, you will find the *twilight zone,* which begins at 650 feet and continues down to 3,250 feet. Leaving the twilight zone, you enter the *bathypelagic zone,* which ends at approximately 19,700 feet below sea level. Anything below 19,700 feet, including the ocean floor, exists in the *hadal zone.*

Take your students on a deep-sea dive through the layers of the ocean. Instruct each student to research the four layers. Then have your junior oceanographers create flip books to record and present their findings. Have each student follow the steps below to create his own "Under the Sea" flip book.

Materials for each student:

Provide each student with markers, crayons, scissors, and one sheet of construction paper in each of the following colors and dimensions:

- white—12" x 5"
- light blue—12" x 7"
- dark blue—12" x 9"
- black—12" x 11"
- brown—12" x 12"

Directions for each student:

Step 1: Carefully trim one 12-inch edge of each sheet of paper (except the brown sheet) in a wavy pattern as shown. No more than one-half inch should be trimmed off. This will form the bottom edge of each page.

Step 2: Stack the colored paper in the following order: white (top sheet), light blue, dark blue, black, and brown (bottom sheet). Be sure that the bottom edge of each sheet is visible as shown.

Step 3: Staple all the sheets together at the top to bind the booklet.

Step 4: The brown, black, dark blue, and light blue pages represent the four layers of the ocean. Label the bottom of each page with the appropriate zone name. On each page, include drawings of plant and animal life found in that zone as well as a brief description of the zone.

Step 5: Decorate the white cover with illustrations and the title "Under the Sea."

DEEP-SEA STATISTICS
Graphing and interpreting data

How deep is the ocean? Divers wearing special pressure suits have been able to dive down to about 1,650 feet. But the ocean is much deeper than that! The average depth of the ocean is about 12,500 feet; however, many ocean basins are 18,000 to 20,000 feet deep. The deepest parts of the ocean are found in *trenches*—long, narrow cracks in the ocean floor found near the edges of continents and island chains.

Help your students learn more about the ocean's deepest trenches. Duplicate page 58 for each student. Then discuss the terms *mean* and *range.* Explain that *mean* is the average of a group of numbers and that *range* is the difference between the greatest and least numbers. Provide students with calculators; then instruct each student to follow the directions on the reproducible. After each student has completed page 58, collect the questions and answers created for the Bonus Box. Use these to help the class discuss the data revealed on the graph.

HIDE AND SEEK
Identifying biological adaptations that affect an organism's survival, creative thinking

Survival is a daily challenge for creatures of the sea. Many sea animals have developed special characteristics that help protect them from predators. Share with your students the following ways various sea creatures hide in the sea:

- **Camouflage**—Camouflage helps animals blend in with their surroundings. Some, like the octopus, even have the ability to change their skin color or texture to match the background.
- **Counter shading**—Dark backs and white stomachs are common characteristics of sea animals. Predators looking up at the animal's white belly have a hard time seeing it against the sunlight reflecting off the water. From above, the animal's dark back blends in with the dark ocean water.
- **Disruptive Coloration**—Some sea creatures, especially ones that live in coral reefs, make use of brightly colored stripes and spots that break up the body shape. This helps conceal them against their backgrounds.
- **False Eye Spots**—Other sea creatures make use of unusual patterns and colors to conceal vulnerable body parts. Some fish have spots that look similar to eyes on the opposite ends of their bodies. This will often confuse predators.

Enlist the aid of your librarian in finding various pictures of sea creatures that use these protective coloration techniques. Show these to your students; then challenge each student to create his own sea creature that makes use of one or all of the camouflaging methods described above. Duplicate page 59 for each student. Instruct each student to follow the directions on the handout. Then have each student present his sea creature to the rest of the class and explain how it hides itself in the sea. Bind the completed pages into a booklet. Add a cover with the title "Now You See Me, Now You Don't!"

IT'S PUZZLING!
Researching endangered animals, recognizing causes of endangerment

Why are certain sea animals in danger? It's a puzzle that many people are trying to solve.

Creating endangered sea animal puzzles is a fun way for students to share information they've gathered about this important topic. Duplicate page 60 for each student and also give each student one 12" x 18" piece of poster board and one 9" x 12" envelope. Then assign each student one of the following threatened or endangered sea animals:

Humpback whale	Steller's sea lion	Brown pelican	California sea lion
Blue whale	Southern sea otter	Abbott's booby	West Indian manatee
Finback whale	Elephant seal	Harbor seal	Galapagos penguin
Sei whale	Sperm whale	Sockeye salmon	Green sea turtle
Gray whale	Bowhead whale	Chinook salmon	Leatherback sea turtle
Right whale	Dugong	Cahow	Loggerhead sea turtle
Roseate tern	Vaquita	American Ridley sea turtle	Saltwater crocodile

Instruct each student to research the information on page 60. After each student has researched his endangered animal and completed page 60, have him glue the reproducible to his poster board. In addition to the reproducible, tell each student to gather magazine pictures, maps, drawings, and words related to his endangered animal and glue them onto his poster. After a student has completed his poster, instruct him to cut it into about 15 jigsaw-puzzle pieces and then place the pieces in the envelope. Tell the student to write the endangered animal's name on the outside of the envelope. When all the puzzles are complete, pass them around the room and have each student complete a different puzzle. Or place the puzzles in a center for students to put together during free time.

Save the Blue Whale

Blue whales are endangered because so many were hunted for oil and other products.

Blue whales have hundreds of thin plates called baleen, which they use to filter krill from the water.

ENDANGERED

54

A DO-IT-YOURSELF OCEAN
Exploring properties of the ocean, making a model

Bring the ocean into the classroom by setting up a saltwater aquarium. An aquarium is a very small environment and not a complete ecosystem, but it will give your students a chance to observe some sea creatures up close. Then recruit a few student volunteers to help you set up the tank. Also enlist students to help with feeding the animals and maintaining the tank. After the tank is complete, have students observe the feeding and resting habits of the various animals in the tank.

Materials:

- 10-gallon (or larger) all-glass or plastic aquarium
- air pump and gravel or box filter
- 50-watt aquarium heater (only if tropical animals are kept in the tank)
- clean marine gravel (enough to cover the bottom of the tank)
- 10 gallons of seawater (or purchase Synthetic Sea Salts—available at most pet supply stores—and follow the directions on the package).

Directions:

1. Find a permanent location for the aquarium away from direct sunlight and heater vents.
2. Use water to rinse the aquarium and anything you plan to put into it. Do not use any soap. Soap residue can harm the animals in the tank.
3. If you have a gravel filter, place it on the bottom of the tank.
4. Cover the bottom of the tank with about two inches of marine gravel.
5. If a box filter is being used, place it on top of the gravel.
6. Connect any air hoses from the filter to the air pump.
7. To keep the gravel in place when the water is poured into the tank, put a piece of plastic wrap on top of it.
8. Slowly pour in seawater. Stop when the water is about an inch from the top.
9. Plug in the pump to aerate the water.
10. Operate the aquarium for two or three days before adding any animals.

Hints:

1. Animals that do well in aquariums include sea urchins, starfish, crabs, shrimp, and a variety of small fish.
2. Many animals in your tank enjoy eating small pieces of squid or brine shrimp.
3. Don't overcrowd your aquarium with sea animals.
4. Replace evaporated seawater with freshwater only. Never use seawater. When the seawater evaporates from the tank, the salt remains. Adding more seawater can make the tank too salty.
5. Murky water indicates bacteria growth. If this occurs, start over with fresh seawater.
6. Remove any sick animals from the tank and place them in a small glass container of seawater; then consult a veterinarian.

Names_____ *Experiment*

Water, Water Everywhere

Imagine that you are the cook on an ocean cruise. Your ship is equipped with a greenhouse for growing food. How will you care for your plants? Can you use seawater to feed them? Complete the experiment below to see what happens when a plant is given salt water.

Materials for each group:
- 2 identical potted plants (4" pots or bigger)
- salt
- water
- measuring cup
- measuring spoon

Hypothesis: What do you think will happen to the plant given salt water? _____
_____

Procedures:
1. Prepare a saltwater mixture by stirring two teaspoons of salt into 1/2 cup of water. Keep this ratio of salt to water throughout the experiment.
2. Label one plant "Salt Water." Give it 1/2 cup of the saltwater mixture every three days for two weeks. Label the second plant "Freshwater." Give it 1/2 cup of freshwater every three days for two weeks.
3. Place both plants in a sunny spot. Observe both plants for 14 days.
4. Record the height, number of leaves, and leaf condition of each plant on the chart below.

Observations: Record observations on the chart below.

		Day 1	Day 4	Day 7	Day 10	Day 14
Salt water	Height:					
	Number of leaves:					
	Leaf condition:					
Freshwater	Height:					
	Number of leaves:					
	Leaf condition:					

Conclusions:
1. What happened to each plant? _____
_____

2. Based on your observations, should you use seawater to water the plants aboard ship?_____
   Explain. _____
_____

Note to the teacher: Duplicate this page for each group to use with "Water, Water Everywhere" on page 51.

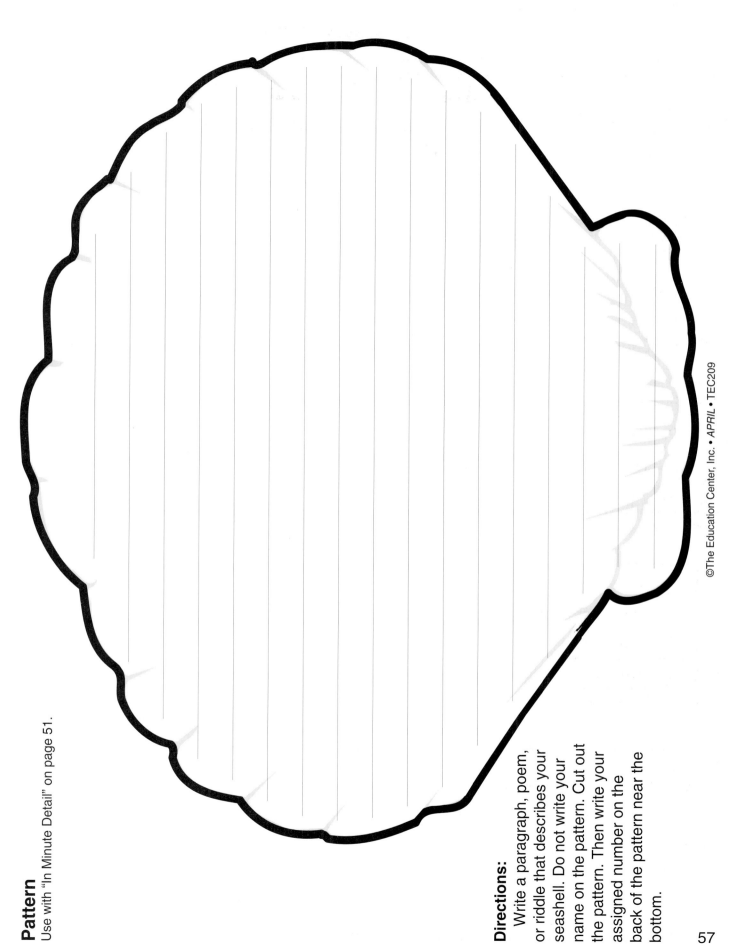

Directions:
   Write a paragraph, poem, or riddle that describes your seashell. Do not write your name on the pattern. Cut out the pattern. Then write your assigned number on the back of the pattern near the bottom.

Name _____

Deep-Sea Statistics

Answer each question below and complete the graph to learn more about the ocean's depths. Use a calculator if needed.

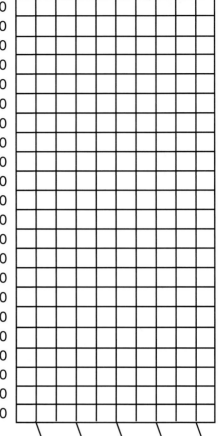

Some of the Deepest Recorded Depths

Puerto Rico Trench—28,374 ft.
Diamantina Depth—26,400 ft.
Mariana Trench—36,198 ft.
Aleutian Trench—25,194 ft.
Cayman Trench—23,288 ft.

1. Number the ocean trenches below in order from the shallowest to the deepest.

    _____ Puerto Rico Trench

    _____ Diamantina Depth

    _____ Mariana Trench

    _____ Aleutian Trench

    _____ Cayman Trench

2. Round each depth to the nearest thousand feet.

    23,288 ft. _____

    25,194 ft. _____

    26,400 ft. _____

    28,374 ft. _____

    36,198 ft. _____

Ocean Depths in Feet

20,000
21,000
22,000
23,000
24,000
25,000
26,000
27,000
28,000
29,000
30,000
31,000
32,000
33,000
34,000
35,000
36,000
37,000
38,000
39,000
40,000
41,000

3. Write the name of each trench or depth along the bottom of the graph as ordered in Step 1.

4. Plot each depth on the graph. Then connect the points to create a line graph showing the rounded depth of each trench.

5. To find the *range* of these depths, subtract the smallest depth from the largest depth.

    _____

6. To find the *mean*, add each rounded depth together; then divide by the number of addends.

    _____

7. Draw a line across the graph identifying the mean depth. How many of the trenches are above the mean? _____ How many are below the mean? _____

Bonus Box: Create five study questions using the line-graph information. Write all five questions and their answers on a sheet of notebook paper.

Hide and Seek

Survival is a daily challenge for creatures of the sea. Many sea animals have adapted special characteristics that help camouflage them from predators. Read the four coloration techniques described below.

- **Camouflage**—Camouflage helps animals blend in with their surroundings. Some, like the octopus, even have the ability to change their skin color or texture to match the background.
- **Counter shading**—Dark backs and white stomachs are common characteristics of sea animals. Predators looking up at the animal's white belly have a hard time seeing it against the sunlight reflecting off the water. From above, the animal's dark back blends in with the dark ocean water.
- **Disruptive Coloration**—Some sea creatures, especially ones that live in coral reefs, make use of brightly colored stripes and spots that break up the body shape. This helps conceal them against their backgrounds.
- **False Eye Spots**—Other sea creatures make use of unusual patterns and colors to conceal vulnerable body parts. Some fish have spots that look similar to eyes on the opposite ends of their bodies. This will often confuse predators.

Directions:

In the box below, create a sea creature that uses one or more of the coloration techniques described above. Be very detailed and specific in your drawing. Fold a sheet of notepaper in half. On the bottom half of the paper, write a brief description of the sea creature. Include information on where it lives in the ocean and how it makes use of the coloration technique(s). Cut out your illustration and glue it to the top of the notepaper.

Bonus Box: If you had the ability to blend in with the background, which coloration technique would you use and when would you use it? Write your response on the back of this page.

Name _____

ENDANGERED

(Write the name of the endangered or threatened animal above.) _____

Why is this animal endangered or threatened? _____
_____
_____

Where does it live? _____
_____
_____

What is being done to remove this animal from the endangered or threatened list? _____
_____
_____

What does it look like? _____
_____
_____

What can you do to help save this animal? _____
_____
_____

What other animals depend on this animal for survival? _____
_____
_____

Note to the teacher: Duplicate this page for each student to use with "It's Puzzling!" on page 54.

Intertidal Zone

A unique strip of land known as the *intertidal zone* exists along the rocky coastline of New England. There the tide rises and falls twice each day. During high tide the land is covered with water. During low tide the land is exposed, leaving many small pools of water in the cracks and crevices known as *tidepools.* Listed below are some of the many sea creatures that live in the intertidal zone. Research to find out what each plant or animal looks like and where it lives in the tidepool. Then create your own intertidal zone in the space below. Be sure to include each sea creature listed below with an identification label in your illustration.

• sea star	• barnacles	• hermit crab	• mussels
• sea lettuce	• sea anemone	• rockfish	• sea cucumber
• sea urchin	• periwinkles	• crabs	• seaweed

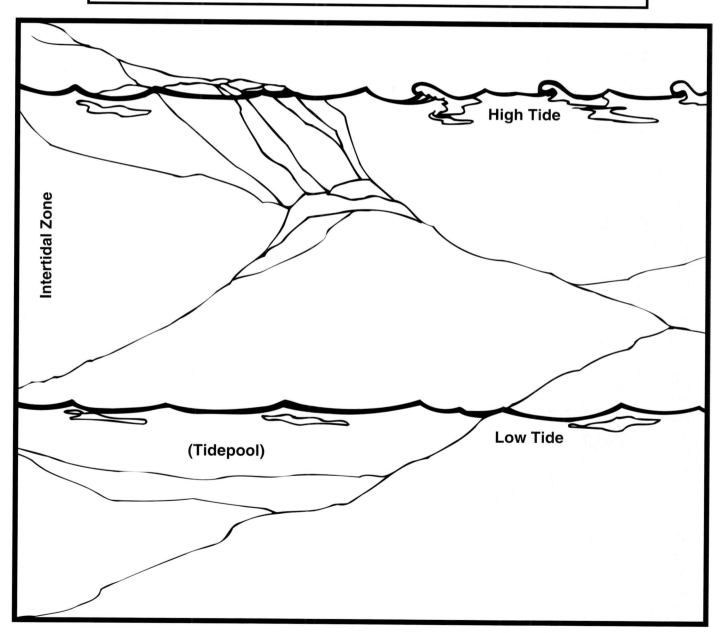

Note to the teacher: Duplicate this page for each student. Assign a due date. Provide students with access to appropriate research materials. Mount each student's completed illustration on a piece of colored paper and display it on a bulletin board or wall.

61

Swing Into BASEBALL

On April 14, 1910, President William Howard Taft started a sports tradition by throwing out the first baseball of the season, helping to make the game a national pastime. So swing into the season with this bonanza of baseball activities!

by Kelly Gooden, Judith Shutter, and Mary Spaulding

Casey at the Bat 🖥
Paraphrasing

Have your students take a swing at paraphrasing with this innovative story-sharing activity! Begin by reading aloud the classic poem "Casey at the Bat" by Ernest Lawrence Thayer. After sharing the poem, divide students into groups. Provide each group with a copy of the poem, seven sheets of connected computer paper, a copy of the baseball-bat pattern on page 69, a yardstick, a thin black marker, and crayons. Challenge each group to reread each of the 13 stanzas of the poem. Then instruct the group to paraphrase each stanza in one sentence. Encourage the group to use the dictionary to look up any unfamiliar words. After all 13 stanzas have been paraphrased, instruct the group to read through its retelling from beginning to end to be sure it makes sense.

Next, give each group the following directions to create an accordion-fold book in which to write its version of the poem:

1. Fold each page of computer paper in half lengthwise to create an accordion fold of the stack. This will create 14 pages (Figure 1).
2. Write the title of the poem and the author on the back of the first page. Below this write "Retold by" and your group members' names.
3. Beginning with page 2, write each story sentence (in correct order) at the top of a different page.
4. Cut out the bat pattern. Glue the handle of the bat halfway down the second page and the top part of the bat halfway down the last page.
5. Open the sheets and use the yardstick and marker to connect the handle of the bat with its top. Color the bat.
6. Add a drawing to illustrate each story sentence.
7. Fold the book back up and punch a hole in the center of the left margin of the stack (Figure 2). Be sure that the hole is punched through all of the sheets of paper.
8. Slip a piece of yarn or ribbon through the hole and tie it to hold the pages in place. Display your version of "Casey at the Bat" for all to enjoy.

Figure 1

Casey at
the Bat
by Ernest
Lawrence Thayer
Retold by
Greg Chopko
Anna Ho
and
Frank Smith

Figure 2

Casey at
the Bat
by Ernest
Lawrence Thayer
Retold by
Greg Chopko
Anna Ho
and
Frank Smith

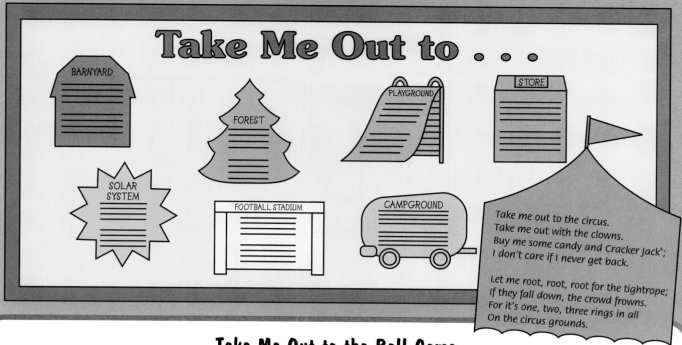

Take Me Out to . . .

BARNYARD

FOREST

PLAYGROUND

STORE

SOLAR SYSTEM

FOOTBALL STADIUM

CAMPGROUND

Take me out to the circus.
Take me out with the clowns.
Buy me some candy and Cracker Jack®;
I don't care if I never get back.

Let me root, root, root for the tightrope;
If they fall down, the crowd frowns.
For it's one, two, three rings in all
On the circus grounds.

Take Me Out to the Ball Game
Writing for a purpose

Have fun with one of the best-known baseball songs around. Ask your music teacher for a recording of the song "Take Me Out to the Ball Game" by Jack Norworth. Write the words of the song on large chart paper so students can sing along as you play the recording. Discuss with students the syllable count, the beat of each line, and the rhyming pattern of the song.

Next, challenge students to change the song's meaning without changing the beat, syllable count, or rhyme. First, have the student choose a new setting for the song, such as a circus, playground, or barnyard. Then have him rewrite the song, changing as many key words as needed to maintain the new meaning. For instance, in the sample above, the two-syllable word *circus* replaces *ball game*. Finally, have each student write his new song on a cutout symbol that represents the setting of his song, such as a tent or an elephant for the circus. Hang the pictures and songs on a bulletin board titled "Take Me Out to…"

Major-League Cities
Researching U.S. cities

Spark a major-league interest in researching U.S. cities. Brainstorm with your students a list of U.S. cities that have a major-league ball club. Use the list on page 66 for help. Then pair students to research the cities. Have each pair look for information about its city, such as area in square miles, population, climate, agriculture, major industries, and tourist attractions (including the baseball stadium). After students complete the research, have each pair create a pennant for its city using a 9" x 12" sheet of construction paper. Direct the pair to write its research information on the back of the pennant. On the front of the pennant, instruct the students to write the city name and design a logo that promotes the city's attributes. After each pair shares its information, hang the pennants on a string that has been stretched at an angle from the classroom ceiling to the floor.

I was treated unfairly one time by my classmates during a ball game. They didn't want me to pitch because I'm a girl. It made me feel bad because I knew I could pitch well. I told them to let me prove to them that I could do a good job. I did! I struck out six opponents. We won the game!

Saved by Baseball
Making a personal connection, explanatory writing

From 1942 to 1945, during World War II, the U.S. Army moved all people of Japanese descent from the West Coast to internment camps in the desert. The U.S. government feared that Japanese Americans might be loyal to Japan. The picture book *Baseball Saved Us,* by Ken Mochizuki, is a moving story about a young boy living in such a camp and his struggle to overcome fear and prejudice. The boy succeeds with the help of baseball.

Read the story aloud to your students. Then have students discuss the following questions: What is prejudice? Do you think the Japanese Americans were treated fairly? Why or why not? Why do you think these people chose baseball to help pass the time during their stay at the camp? How do you think you would feel if you were in this type of situation?

Follow up by giving each student a copy of page 69 and a sheet of white paper. Direct the student to cut out the baseball-bat sections and then tape each section to a different end of the white paper. Next, have her cut the white paper to create the center portion of the bat. Challenge the student to think of a time when she experienced prejudice or a situation in which she was treated unfairly. Encourage her to write an explanation of how she handled the situation and to tell what she learned from the experience. On the bat pattern, have her write her final draft and include an illustration. Display the stories on a wall or bulletin board titled "Home Run Stories."

From the Box
Reading and interpreting tables, participating in an oral presentation

Want to find out if you have the next Al Michaels sitting in your classroom? To be a good sports reporter, you need to have all of the facts. One way to get the facts about a baseball game is by reading a *box score*. A box score gives a statistical summary of a baseball game. It can be found in the sports section of a newspaper.

Familiarize your students with a sample box score and its abbreviations by giving each pair of students a copy of page 67. Have the pair use the abbreviation key and the box score on the sheet to answer the questions about the game. Next, give each pair a different copy of a box score that you have previously clipped from a newspaper. Have the partners answer ten questions about the game's statistics, such as the following: Who played the game? What were the total runs scored per inning? Who won the game? What was the final score?

Instruct the pair to also write about highlights of the game, such as double plays, triple plays, home runs, bases stolen, and a pitching summary. Show students a videotape of a sports newscast to help them visualize a report. Then have each pair share its information by role-playing a sports-caster's report.

HOME RUN

No-Strikes Spelling
Reviewing spelling skills

Step up to the plate with this winning vocabulary game! Before you begin the game, label index cards with one letter of the alphabet on each card. Create extra letter cards as needed for words on your vocabulary list that contain more than one of the same letter. Next, divide your students into teams of five or six. Have one team at a time stand in front of the room, ready to use the index cards to spell out a word. Call out a word from your vocabulary list. Instruct the team members to find the appropriate letters and then hold up the cards, spelling the word correctly. Have the rest of the class act as umpires. Direct them to act out the *safe* signal that is used in baseball if the word is spelled correctly, and the *out* signal that is used in baseball if it is spelled incorrectly. Give each team three chances to spell the word correctly. If a team strikes out, allow the students on that team to act only as umpires for the remainder of the game, and pass the word to the next team. If the team spells the word correctly, have its members remain in the game and wait for their next turn. Play the game until all words are spelled correctly; then give a rousing cheer for the winning teams.

Spin to Win
Understanding probability, conducting an experiment

What are the odds that a favorite team will win the World Series? Help your students gain an understanding of probability by letting them experiment with *odds*. Begin by explaining that probability involves making predictions based on a number of outcomes. For example, if a spinner has three possible outcomes, then the theory is that there is a one-in-three chance that any outcome will happen. The theory can then be tested by conducting experiments. Have each of your students conduct her own experiment with probability. Give each student a copy of page 68. Have her use a paper clip and a pencil to find out more.

On the Road! 🖵
Reviewing map skills

Follow the road to geography fun with this map skills activity! On a wall or bulletin board, display the American and National League lists below along with a large U.S.-Canada map. Help students review map skills, such as using cardinal directions, interpreting a key, using a grid to find places, and figuring mileage. Then follow the directions below to help your students use these skills.

1. Select six teams and a destination for each.
2. Create a road trip schedule as shown below for each team. You provide the information for statements 1, 3, and 4. The students complete the information for statement 2.
3. Group students into teams of four or five, and assign each team either an American or National League team name.
4. Give each team a copy of the baseball-cap pattern on page 69, its road trip schedule, a piece of yarn, tape, and two tacks. Direct the team to label the cap with the team name and then cut it out. Next, tell the team to identify its home city on the map and tape the cap to the edge of the map. Then have the team use the yarn and tacks to connect the cap to its city.
5. Have each team use the map to determine how to get to its destination. After recording its answer on the schedule, have the team cut out and tack the schedule next to the team cap.
6. Extend the activity by having each team create and determine other road trip schedules.

American League	National League
Anaheim Angels	Arizona Diamondbacks
Baltimore Orioles	Atlanta Braves
Boston Red Sox	Chicago Cubs
Chicago White Sox	Cincinnati Reds
Cleveland Indians	Colorado Rockies
Detroit Tigers	Florida Marlins
Kansas City Royals	Houston Astros
Minnesota Twins	Los Angeles Dodgers
New York Yankees	Milwaukee Brewers
Oakland A's	Montreal Expos
Seattle Mariners	New York Mets
Tampa Bay Devil Rays	Philadelphia Phillies
Texas Rangers	Pittsburgh Pirates
Toronto Blue Jays	San Diego Padres
	San Francisco Giants
	St. Louis Cardinals

Hall of Famers 🖵
Collecting and graphing data

Who are your future baseball Hall of Famers? Have students take several bats and softballs, a stopwatch, a measuring tape, and lots of energy out to the school's ball field to test their skills. Give one copy of the "Personal Bests" record sheet below to each child. After warming up and practicing each event, begin to test each student, giving him three tries at each event. Test each student for speed in running to first base, for ability to hit the ball, for strength and accuracy in throwing, and for skill in catching a ball. Have each student record the results and determine his average on his record sheet.

Follow up the activity by creating a large bar graph for each of the four events. Direct each student to record his average on each of the graphs. Vary the activity by dividing the class into four groups, and have each group determine a class average for one of the events. Hang the graphs on a wall or bulletin board titled "Our Future Hall of Famers!"

Road Trip Schedule
1. Your team is the **Mets.**
2. The team travels west for 135 miles.
3. Your destination is **Philadelphia.**
4. Your opponents are the **Phillies.**

Personal Bests				
Activity	1	2	3	Average
Run to First				
Hit or Miss				
Ball Throw				
Catch or Miss				

From the Box

The ball game between the Wrens and the Cats was awesome—but you missed it! Use this **box score** summary to get the facts about the game and to help you answer the questions that follow. Write your answers on the back of this sheet.

Box Score

Wrens

	ab	r	h	bi
Jones, cf	5	0	1	0
Smith, rf	5	2	2	1
Collins, ss	5	0	0	0
Brown, p	5	1	2	1
Peters, 1b	5	0	1	0
Cole, 2b	3	0	1	1
Stevens, c	3	1	1	0
Brady, lf	4	1	2	2
King, 3b	4	0	0	0
Totals	**39**	**5**	**10**	**5**

Cats

	ab	r	h	bi
White, rf	4	0	0	1
Adams, lf	4	0	0	0
Reed, ss	4	0	1	0
Bush, p	3	0	0	0
Young, 1b	4	0	1	0
Wood, 2b	4	0	2	0
Green, 3b	4	0	0	0
Marsh, cf	4	1	1	0
Towner, c	3	1	2	0
Totals	**34**	**2**	**7**	**1**

> This part of the box gives player names, positions, and game statistics.

Wrens	010	012	001—5
Cats	002	000	000—2

> This part of the box summarizes the runs per inning and total runs.

DP–Wrens 1. LOB–Wrens 9, Cats 6. HR–Brady, Smith. 2B–Smith, Brown, Stevens, Wood, Towner.

	IP	H	ER	BB	SO
Wrens					
Brown (W, 8-7)	9	7	2	1	7
Cats					
Bush (L, 4-5)	9	10	5	2	6

T–2:59 A–38,086

> This part of the box gives game statistics and a pitching summary.

Abbreviations

ab	times at bat		W	winning pitcher and won-lost record
r	runs scored			
h	base hits			
bi	runs batted in		L	losing pitcher and won-lost record
E	errors			
DP	double play		T	time of game
LOB	runners left on base		A	paid attendance
2B	doubles		cf	center field
3B	triples		rf	right field
HR	home runs		ss	shortstop
SB	stolen bases		p	pitcher
IP	innings pitched		1b	first base
H	base hits allowed		2b	second base
ER	earned runs allowed		c	catcher
BB	base on balls		lf	left field
SO	strikeouts		3b	third base

Coach's Quiz

1. Who played first base for the Wrens? Who played first base for the Cats?
2. How many times did Cole go to bat?
3. Who scored more runs, Smith or Marsh?
4. The Wrens scored how many more base hits than the Cats?
5. Which team won the game, and what was the final score?
6. How many innings were played during the game?
7. Which players scored home runs?
8. The Wrens' pitcher struck out how many of the Cats' players?
9. How long did the game last?
10. How many paying fans attended the game?

Bonus Box: Use the box score to create 5 of your own questions for a classmate to answer.

Spin to Win

What are the odds that your favorite team will win the World Series? Experiment with probability using the activity below. Before you begin, write the name of your favorite baseball team in space number 1 on each spinner below. Then fill in the other spinner spaces with other team names. To spin, place a pencil point inside the end of a paper clip and on the center of the spinner. Flick the other end of the clip and watch where it lands.

Spinner 1

1. The probability of the spinner landing on space number 1 is _____.
2. The probability of the spinner *not* landing on space number 1 is _____.
3. My prediction: I will land on space number 1 _____ times out of 30 spins.
4. Try it out. Tally each spin below.

1	2	3

5. I landed on space number 1 _____ times.
6. I did *not* land on space number 1 _____ times.

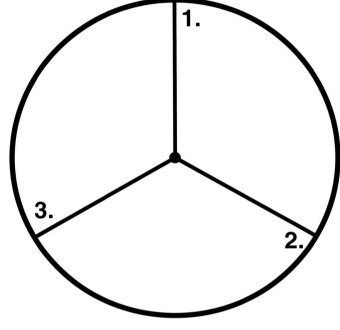

Spinner 2

1. The probability of the spinner landing on space number 1 is _____.
2. The probability of the spinner *not* landing on space number 1 is _____.
3. My prediction: I will land on space number 1 _____ times out of 60 spins.
4. Try it out. Tally each spin below.

1	2	3	4	5	6

5. I landed on space number 1 _____ times.
6. I did *not* land on space number 1 _____ times.

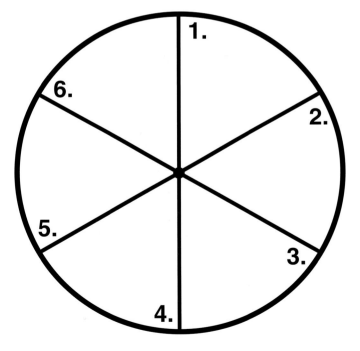

Bonus Box: Make a third spinner with 12 spaces. Think of the probability of landing on numerous spaces, such as the probability of landing on the spaces with odd numbers. Make your predictions and try them out!

Patterns

Use with "Casey at the Bat" on page 62 and "Saved by Baseball" on page 64.

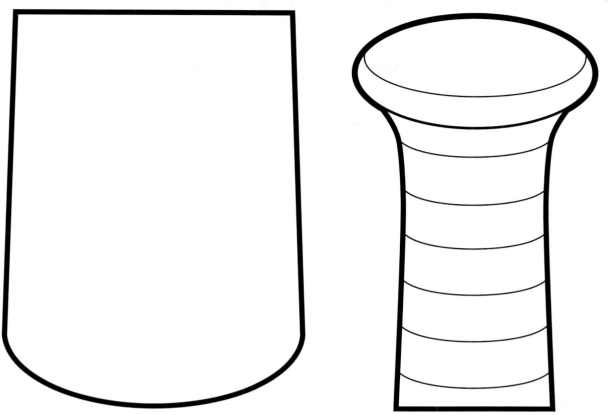

Use with "On the Road!" on page 66.

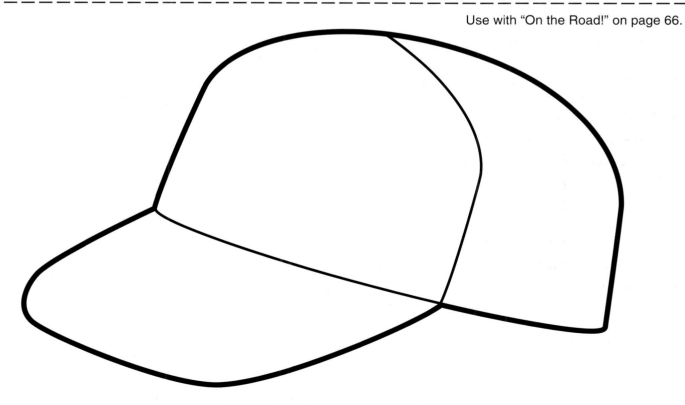

Money:
Ideas You Can Bank On

Activities for Exploring Money Concepts With Your Students

The first U.S. Mint was established in Philadelphia, Pennsylvania, on April 2, 1792. But money was an important part of everyday life long before that important date. Incorporate this unit's cross-curricular ideas into your lessons to cash in on the educational value of money.

by Marsha Schmus, Debra Liverman, and Stephanie Willett-Smith

Writing That's Worth a Million
Expressive writing

Get your students motivated with this million-dollar writing activity! Have each student imagine what her life would be like if she had a million dollars. To illustrate the concept of a million, ask a student volunteer to locate Philadelphia, Pennsylvania, and New York, New York, on a U.S. map. Point out that 1,000,000 one-dollar bills laid end to end would be equal to the distance between these two cities.

Then have each student imagine that she has just made a million-dollar profit through smart money investments. Instruct each student to write a story that tells how she would use her fortune. Use the pattern on page 76 as a cover for the story. Add a personal touch by having the student mount a photo or drawing of herself in the empty space on the pattern. Display the completed stories on a bulletin board as shown.

Making Some Changes
Calculating change, logical thinking
Everyone needs to know how to make correct change. Review some common ways to make change for a dollar with your students, such as four quarters or ten dimes or 20 nickels. Then challenge students to give examples of other, more creative ways to make change, such as using five pennies, two dimes, and three quarters. Afterward, have students work in teams to come up with as many ways as possible to make change for a dollar. Write some of these combinations on the board. For additional practice with making change, duplicate page 78 for students to complete.

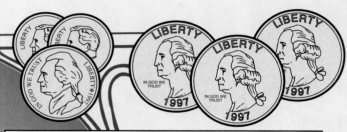

Dream Bedroom Expense Graph

Cost of Dream Bedroom Items
(in dollars)

200 —
175 —
150 —
125 —
100 —
75 —
50 —
25 —
0 —

Jake   Bill   Kim   Ann

Students—Group A

Shop 'til You Drop
Collecting, graphing, and interpreting data
Is there anything more exciting than an all-expenses-paid shopping trip? Tell your class that money is no object for this assignment! Allow each student to look through old catalogs and sale circulars to select items he would like for his dream bedroom. Remind him not to forget such essentials as sheets, pillows, hangers, and other small items. Have the student cut out each item he selects for purchase, along with its price, and mount these items on a piece of construction paper. Then instruct the student to calculate the total cost of the items and record this total on his paper.

Next, divide the class into groups of four or five students. Have each group create a bar graph, as shown, to compare group members' total costs. Instruct each group to note whose bedroom was the cheapest and whose was the most expensive, and then calculate the average cost of all the group members' bedrooms. Finally, have each group present its graph and findings to the class. You can bet your bottom dollar that your students will enjoy showing off their purchases for all to see!

Money Belts 🖥

Experiencing a cultural tradition

What is *money?* When most people think of money, they picture bills and coins—much like our system of currency. But money can take many forms. *Money* is defined as "anything accepted as a method of payment." In the past, people have used cocoa beans, shells, stones, tobacco, salt, beads, copper, silver, and gold as money. *Wampum*—white and purple beads made from shells—were originally used by Native Americans for sending messages and recording treaties and histories. The wampum beads were often strung into decorative belts. When European settlers saw how much the Native Americans valued wampum, they began using it as money. Give your students a hands-on opportunity to explore alternative money by allowing them to make their own wampum belts.

Fig. 1

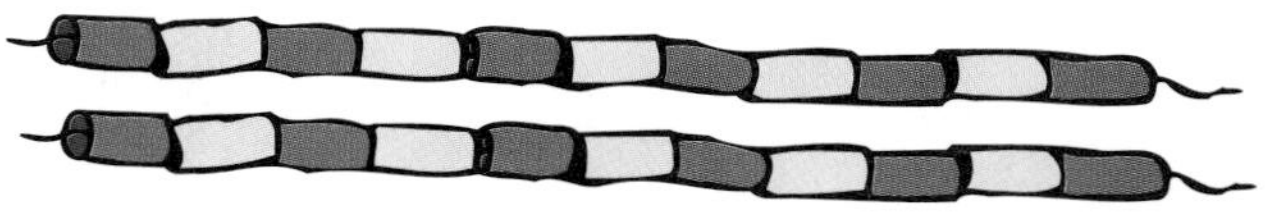

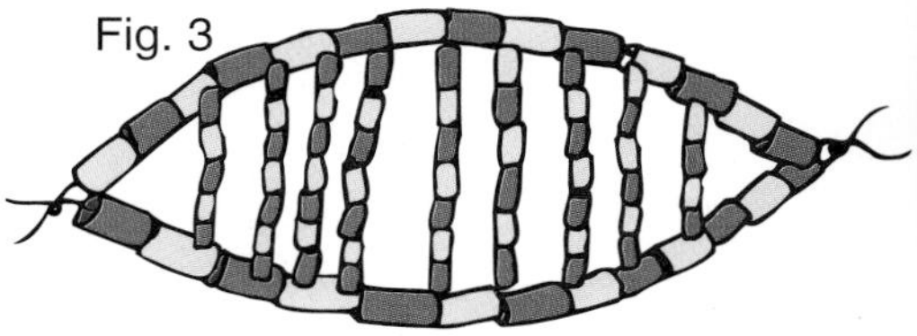

Materials:
two 16 oz. bags of ditalini pasta noodles
red and blue food coloring
1/3 c. rubbing alcohol
large mixing bowl
paper towels
two 36 in. lengths of yarn per student
nine 5 in. lengths of yarn per student
eighteen 10 in. lengths of yarn per student (for tassels)

Fig. 2

Directions:
1. In the bowl, mix the alcohol, six drops of blue food coloring, and ten drops of red food coloring.
2. Pour one 16-ounce bag of noodles into the mixture.
3. Stir the mixture with a spoon until noodles are coated with color. For darker color, allow the noodles to soak for additional time.
4. Spread the noodles on paper towels to dry.
5. Use undyed noodles to represent the white wampum beads.

Fig. 3

Student directions for constructing wampum belts:
1. String the purple and white noodles on each 36-inch length of yarn to make a pattern (Figure 1).
2. Tie these two decorated strands together at each end to secure the noodles in place and make a two-strand belt (Figure 2).
3. String noodles on each of the nine five-inch lengths.
4. Tie the ends of the completed five-inch lengths at equally spaced points on both of the two 36-inch strands to act as spacers for the longer pieces (Figure 3).
5. Use the remaining eighteen ten-inch lengths of yarn to create decorative tassels for the belt's ends. For each tassel, lay seven ten-inch lengths side by side. Take another length of yarn and lay it across the middle of these lengths. Fold the bundle of lengths in half and secure it about one inch from the fold using an additional piece of yarn (Figures 4–6). Repeat this procedure to make the second tassel. Tie one tassel to each end of the belt (Figure 7).
6. Display your wampum belt or give it to another student as a sign of friendship.

Fig. 4

Fig. 5    **Fig. 6**

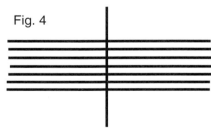

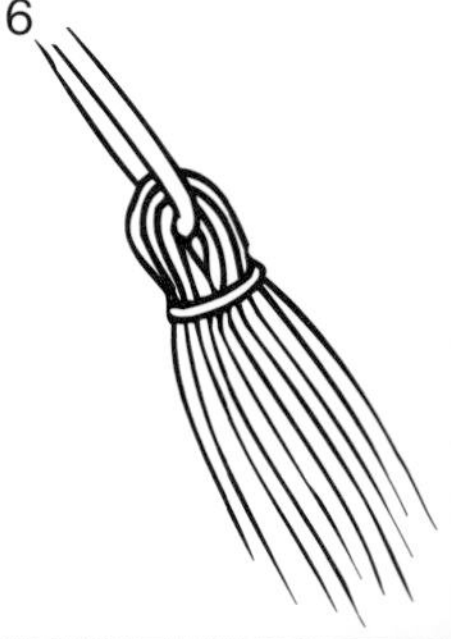

Fig. 7

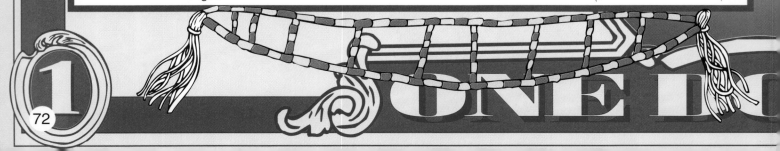

A Penny for Your Thoughts 🖥
Understanding figurative language

References to money are found throughout our language. Have your students brainstorm sayings that refer to money, and record their suggestions on a piece of chart paper. Some common money-related phrases include the following:

- pay through the nose
- a penny for your thoughts
- penny-pincher
- penny-wise and pound-foolish
- pass the buck
- red cent
- two cents worth
- look like a million bucks
- bet your bottom dollar
- cash in on
- cash on the barrelhead
- costs an arm and a leg
- a dime a dozen
- money is no object
- money to burn
- in the chips
- made of money
- run for the money
- money burns a hole in your pocket
- put money on a scratched horse
- worth a cent
- coin money
- mint money

Cut out two five-inch light brown circles (coins) for each student. Have the student choose a money phrase and write an explanation of its figurative meaning on one of his circles. On his other circle, direct the student to illustrate the phrase based on its literal meaning. In the center of a bulletin board, display a large piggy bank cutout. Arrange the coins and the title as shown.

Commemorative Class Coins
Understanding the U.S. monetary system, creative thinking

Highlight the important events of the school year by having students design commemorative coins. Explain that, in addition to coins for general circulation, the U.S. Mint makes commemorative coins to celebrate a variety of special occasions. Bring in several examples of coins minted by the U.S. Mint. Discuss the features that make each of the sample coins unique. Ask students to brainstorm memorable events and activities from the current school year, such as a special field trip, holiday program, or novel that was shared. Record these student suggestions on the board.

Have each student select an event from the list and design a commemorative coin similar to a sample coin. Remind the student that a different design is needed for each side of the coin. Provide each student with a piece of round cardboard 12 inches in diameter on which to make the final version of her coin. Hang the finished commemorative coins from the ceiling in your classroom. Students will appreciate the chance to put in their two cents worth.

Cash In on These Money Phrases!

If something is a dime a dozen, then it's very common.

1 Dozen cookies

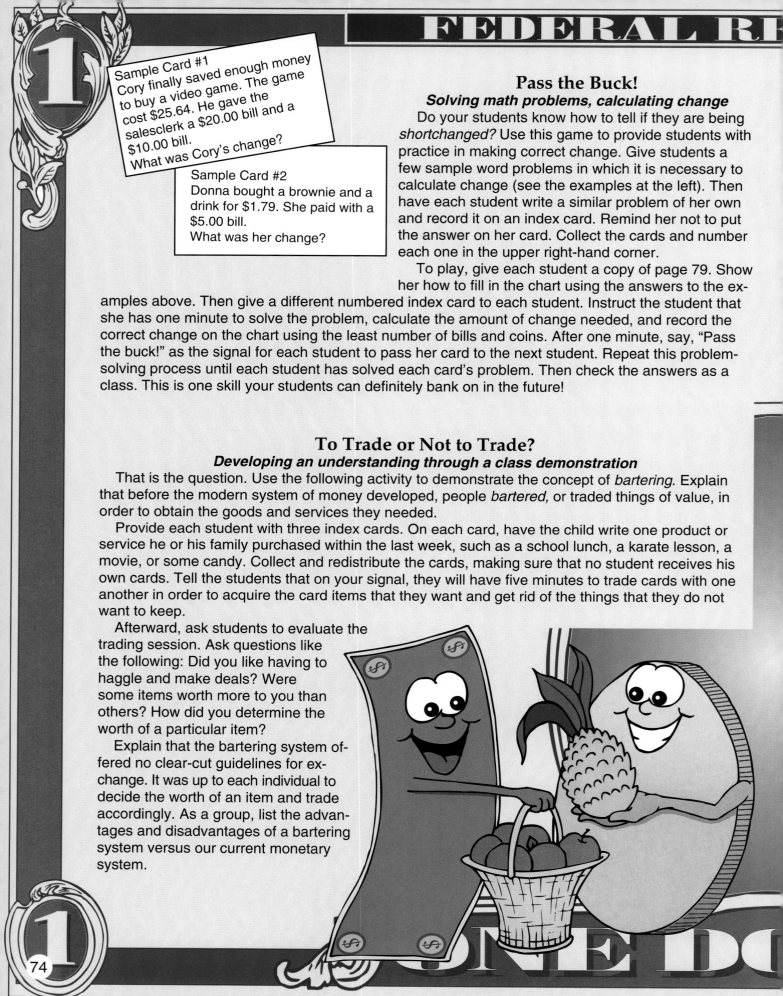

Sample Card #1
Cory finally saved enough money to buy a video game. The game cost $25.64. He gave the salesclerk a $20.00 bill and a $10.00 bill.
What was Cory's change?

Sample Card #2
Donna bought a brownie and a drink for $1.79. She paid with a $5.00 bill.
What was her change?

Pass the Buck!
Solving math problems, calculating change

Do your students know how to tell if they are being *shortchanged?* Use this game to provide students with practice in making correct change. Give students a few sample word problems in which it is necessary to calculate change (see the examples at the left). Then have each student write a similar problem of her own and record it on an index card. Remind her not to put the answer on her card. Collect the cards and number each one in the upper right-hand corner.

To play, give each student a copy of page 79. Show her how to fill in the chart using the answers to the examples above. Then give a different numbered index card to each student. Instruct the student that she has one minute to solve the problem, calculate the amount of change needed, and record the correct change on the chart using the least number of bills and coins. After one minute, say, "Pass the buck!" as the signal for each student to pass her card to the next student. Repeat this problem-solving process until each student has solved each card's problem. Then check the answers as a class. This is one skill your students can definitely bank on in the future!

To Trade or Not to Trade?
Developing an understanding through a class demonstration

That is the question. Use the following activity to demonstrate the concept of *bartering*. Explain that before the modern system of money developed, people *bartered,* or traded things of value, in order to obtain the goods and services they needed.

Provide each student with three index cards. On each card, have the child write one product or service he or his family purchased within the last week, such as a school lunch, a karate lesson, a movie, or some candy. Collect and redistribute the cards, making sure that no student receives his own cards. Tell the students that on your signal, they will have five minutes to trade cards with one another in order to acquire the card items that they want and get rid of the things that they do not want to keep.

Afterward, ask students to evaluate the trading session. Ask questions like the following: Did you like having to haggle and make deals? Were some items worth more to you than others? How did you determine the worth of a particular item?

Explain that the bartering system offered no clear-cut guidelines for exchange. It was up to each individual to decide the worth of an item and trade accordingly. As a group, list the advantages and disadvantages of a bartering system versus our current monetary system.

ONE DO

Classroom Currency
Developing an understanding through a class demonstration

Cash in on this opportunity to demonstrate the basic flow of money in the economy of a society. Create play money and use it as the basis for your own classroom's economy. Have your students help design this currency by copying a reproducible money pattern and inserting your principal's photo. Be sure to create a variety of denominations.

Point out that in an economy, people exchange money for goods and services. As a class, determine a set of costs for certain classroom jobs and services. For one week, use the play money to pay your students for the jobs they complete. Vary the amount of pay depending on the job completed and the length of service. Also require a student to pay money when he is the recipient of a service or product. Offer additional goods for students to purchase, such as a pencil, computer time, lunch with the teacher, or extra recess. Your students will quickly learn that most people don't have money to burn!

High Rollers
Calculating money, understanding place value

Your students will be "die-ing" to play this game and will get practice adding money while working on place value. Divide your class into groups of two to four players. Give each player a gameboard like the one pictured below. In addition, provide each group with a die, a calculator, and the following directions:

To play:
Player A:
a. Roll the die and record that number in the upper half of one of the five blanks in the Round 1 row.
b. Roll the die four more times and record each number rolled until all the spaces in the Round 1 row are filled.
c. Using your calculator, multiply the number rolled by the value listed at the top of the column. Write that product in the lower half of each blank.
d. Add the five products of that round together to get the final total. Write that total in the Total column.

Players B, C, and D: In turn, complete the same steps as Player A. Continue in the same manner for Rounds 2, 3, and 4.

At the end of each round, compare the players' totals. The player with the largest total wins the round.

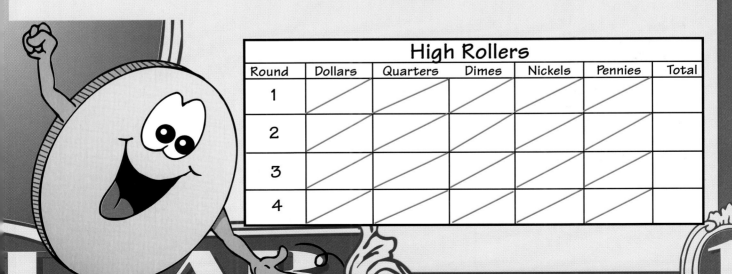

High Rollers

Round	Dollars	Quarters	Dimes	Nickels	Pennies	Total
1						
2						
3						
4						

Money Makes the World Go Round
Researching currencies

Use the following research activity to familiarize your students with the various units of money used in countries around the globe. List several countries—organized by continent—on your chalkboard (see the list below). Assign each student a country to research. Have him look up the currency and flag of his assigned nation. Then have him draw the flag on an unlined index card and label the card with the name of the country and its basic unit of currency. Post these index cards around the perimeter of a large map of the world. Use yarn to match each card to its country on the map. Your students will be amazed at the wide variety of currency used in our world!

Suggested countries and their currencies include the following:

Europe
Ireland—*pound*
United Kingdom—*pound*
Norway—*krone*
Denmark—*krone*
Finland—*markka*
Sweden—*krona*
France—*franc*
Germany—*Deutsche mark*
Netherlands—*gulden*
Switzerland—*frank/franc*
Russia—*ruble*

North America
Canada—*dollar*
United States—*dollar*
Mexico—*peso*

South America
Peru—*inti*
Ecuador—*sucre*
Brazil—*cruzado*
Chile—*peso*
Argentina—*australes*

Australia
Australia—*dollar*

Asia
India—*rupee*
Japan—*yen*
Sri Lanka—*rupee*
Iran—*rial*
China—*yuan*
Thailand—*baht*

Africa
Egypt—*pound*
Ethiopia—*birr*
South Africa—*rand*
Nigeria—*naira*

Ethiopia

(birr)

Story Cover Pattern
Use with "Writing That's Worth a Million" on page 70.

©The Education Center, Inc. • APRIL • TEC209

76

Tic-Tac-Total

To play this game, you need a partner and a pencil.

How to play: Select a gameboard below for the first round of play.

Player 1:
1. Select 2 items to purchase.
2. Round the price of each item to the nearest dollar.
3. Mentally add the rounded numbers together to estimate their total cost. For example, if you pick a football for $10.19 and a soccer ball for $8.99, add the rounded totals of $10.00 and $9.00 to get $19.00.
4. Look at the totals on the Tic-Tac-Total board you selected for this round. If your total is on that board, mark it with an *X* or an *O,* depending on your letter.

Player 2:
1. Follow steps 1–4 above.
2. If your correct estimated total is already taken, you cannot make a mark, and you lose your turn.
3. Continue play in the same manner until 1 player has marked 3 *X*s or *O*s in a line.
4. Then choose a new gameboard and begin a new game.

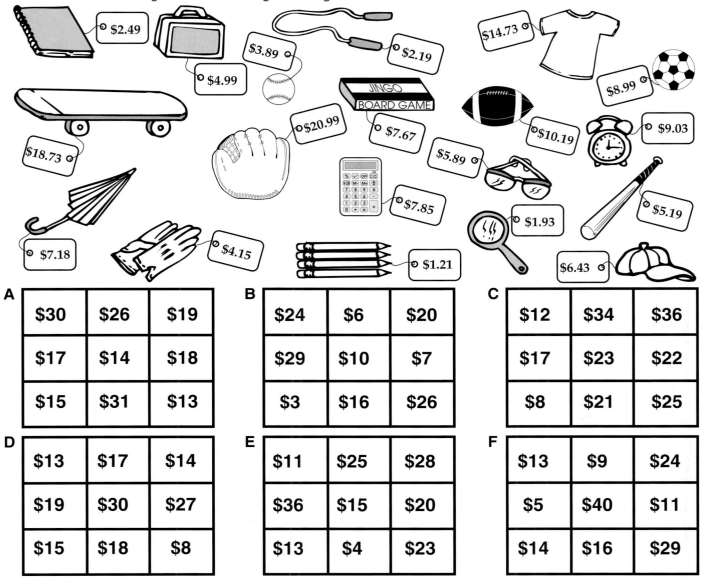

A		
$30	$26	$19
$17	$14	$18
$15	$31	$13

B		
$24	$6	$20
$29	$10	$7
$3	$16	$26

C		
$12	$34	$36
$17	$23	$22
$8	$21	$25

D		
$13	$17	$14
$19	$30	$27
$15	$18	$8

E		
$11	$25	$28
$36	$15	$20
$13	$4	$23

F		
$13	$9	$24
$5	$40	$11
$14	$16	$29

Bonus Box: Design a similar Tic-Tac-Total board on the back of this sheet.

©The Education Center, Inc. • *APRIL* • TEC209

Note to the teacher: Duplicate this page for each pair of students. Each student needs a pencil.

 # Spring Carnival

You have been asked to work the change booth at your school's spring carnival. Your job is to make change for people so they can play the games. Use your money mastery to solve these problems.

1. Jaime wants 16 coins for $1.00. He asks for 2 quarters, plus some dimes and pennies. Give him the correct change.

   _____ pennies

   _____ dimes

   2 quarters

2. Marie asks for 28 coins for $1.00. She wants 15 pennies and some dimes and nickels. Calculate the correct change.

   15 pennies

   _____ nickels

   _____ dimes

3. Bill wants 24 coins for his dollar. He requests 7 nickels. He also wants pennies and quarters. What is his change?

   _____ pennies

   7 nickels

   _____ quarters

4. Consuela would like 10 coins for her dollar. She wants 1 quarter, some dimes, and some nickels. Give her the correct change.

   _____ nickels

   _____ dimes

   1 quarter

5. Carrie needs 17 coins for her dollar. She wants 2 quarters and some dimes, nickels, and pennies. Figure out her correct change.

   _____ pennies

   _____ nickels

   _____ dimes

   2 quarters

6. Sharon wants to trade her dollar in for 19 coins. She wants 5 dimes, 1 quarter, and some nickels and pennies. What is her change?

   _____ pennies

   _____ nickels

   5 dimes

   1 quarter

Bonus Box: On the back of this sheet, write 2 problems similar to the ones above.

Pass the Buck!

Directions: Solve the problem on the index card you receive. Record the answer below on the line with the same number as the number written in the upper right-hand corner of the card. When your teacher says, "Pass the buck," pass the index card to the person next to you. Keep this sheet to work the next problem that is passed to you.

CARD NUMBER	$20 BILLS	$10 BILLS	$5 BILLS	$1 BILLS	QUARTERS	DIMES	NICKELS	PENNIES	TOTAL CHANGE
Sample Card 1				4	1	1		1	$4.36
Sample Card 2				3		2		1	$3.21
1									
2									
3									
4									
5									
6									
7									
8									
9									
10									
11									
12									
13									
14									
15									
16									
17									
18									
19									
20									
21									
22									
23									
24									
25									

Bonus Box: On the back of this sheet, write 10 different ways to make change for a $100 bill.

Note to the teacher: Use this page with "Pass the Buck!" on page 74.

Name _____

Put Your Money Where Your Mouth Is!

Do you know how much the words you speak daily are worth? Find out with this costly activity.

Directions: In this activity, each letter of the alphabet has a monetary value. *A* is worth $1, *B* is worth $2, *C* is worth $3, and so on. Fill in the grid below with the value of each letter. Then use the grid to help you solve the problems below.

A	B	C	D	E	F	G	H	I	J	K	L	M	N	O	P	Q	R	S	T	U	V	W	X	Y	Z
$1	$2	$3																							

1. What is the value of your first name? _____

2. Write a word that is worth less than $25.00. _____

3. What is the value of your birth month? _____

4. What is the difference between the values of your first and last names? _____

5. Write someone's name that is worth $5.00 more than yours. _____

6. What is the value of your teacher's last name? _____

7. What is the value of your school's name? _____

8. Calculate the value of your best friend's first name. _____

9. What is the value of your favorite color? _____

10. Calculate the value of your favorite holiday. _____

Bonus Box: Calculate the total value of the entire alphabet.

Garage Sale Extravaganza!

The Salem Woods Homeowners' Association is sponsoring a neighborhood yard sale for its residents. Several families have decided to participate in the sale to get rid of the junk they have collected over the years. To attract customers, the families have decided to advertise their individual sales in local newspapers. Help each family calculate the costs of advertising by using the information below. The maximum number of characters per line in each paper is 25.

- *The Sun* charges $1.00 per line for 3 days of advertising.
- *The Evening Post* charges $0.75 per line for the first 2 days. For each additional day of advertising, it charges $0.20 per line.

---

1. Mr. and Mrs. Marshall want this ad to run for 3 days.

   Garage Sale—Saturday
   9:00–3:00
   Toys, books, clothes,
   and sporting equipment.
   1407 Pissarro Circle
   Follow the orange signs!

   Calculate the cost of running the ad in each paper.

   The Sun _____
   The Evening Post _____

2. Which paper will run the Marshalls' ad at the cheaper price? _____

---

3. The Rose family wants the following ad to run for 6 days:

   Garage Sale on Saturday
   Something for everyone.
   Come early to get the best deals!
   7:00–1:30
   1532 Degas Court

   Calculate the cost of running the ad in each paper.

   The Sun _____
   The Evening Post _____

4. What will the Roses' total cost be for running the ad in both papers for 6 days?

   _____

---

5. The Riveras want to run this ad for 9 days.

   Don't Miss Out!
   Garage Sale Saturday
   BARGAINS Galore!
   2335 Summerwalk Drive
   8:00–2:30

   Calculate the cost of running the ad in each paper.

   The Sun _____
   The Evening Post _____

6. The Riveras want to run their ad in both papers for 9 days. What will their total cost be?

   _____

---

7. The McLaughlins have decided to run the following ad for 6 days:

   Huge Garage Sale
   Saturday: 7–3
   Baby Items, Toys,
   Children's Clothes,
   Furniture, Crafts.
   Much, Much More!
   2378 Willimantic Court

   Calculate the cost of running the ad in each paper.
   The Sun _____
   The Evening Post _____

8. In which paper will it be more economical for the McLaughlins to run their ad?

   _____

Bonus Box: Write your own garage sale advertisement. Be sure to include the time and location of your sale. Tell how long and in which paper(s) your ad will run and what your total cost will be.

Planning the Perfect Picnic!

Plan an end-of-the-year picnic your class will never forget! There are 24 people attending the picnic, including your teacher, the chaperones, and yourself. The class has voted and decided to serve hot dogs and buns, Doritos®, Coca-Cola®, and cupcakes. You will also need to buy ketchup, mustard, paper plates, and napkins. The chaperones have agreed to supply the ice and grilling supplies. You'll want to do your shopping for the rest of the supplies at Newton's Grocery because it has the best prices.

As picnic coordinator, you must
- plan how much food to buy—supplying 1 of each menu item per person
- calculate the total cost for the picnic using the advertisement from Newton's Grocery
- calculate how much each person needs to pay

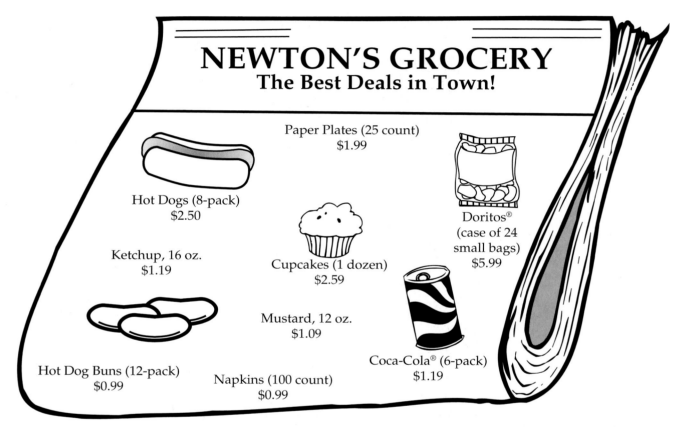

NEWTON'S GROCERY
The Best Deals in Town!

Paper Plates (25 count)
$1.99

Hot Dogs (8-pack)
$2.50

Doritos®
(case of 24
small bags)
$5.99

Ketchup, 16 oz.
$1.19

Cupcakes (1 dozen)
$2.59

Mustard, 12 oz.
$1.09

Hot Dog Buns (12-pack)
$0.99

Napkins (100 count)
$0.99

Coca-Cola® (6-pack)
$1.19

Item	Cost	# Needed	Subtotal	Item	Cost	# Needed	Subtotal
				Grand Total (not including tax)			
				Cost per Person			

Bonus Box: Write a letter to parents detailing your plans for the picnic. Be sure to mention how much money each person will need to bring.

A Tribute to Trees

Founded in 1872 by Julius Sterling Morton of Nebraska, Arbor Day is a holiday that recognizes the importance of trees in our past and in our future. Use the following innovative activities to pay tribute to these truly magnificent plants—trees.

by Patricia Altmann, Cindy Mondello, and Elizabeth Tanzi

Crowning Achievements
Identifying character traits, making a personal connection

The leaves of a tree help feed and nourish the tree as it grows, while the branches offer it support and strength. Together, this crown of leaves and branches provides the environment with protection and beauty. In a similar way, you and your students have qualities that make up unique branches of your "classroom tree." Illustrate this concept for your students by cutting a large tree out of brown paper and arranging it on a bulletin board as shown. Label the trunk of the tree with your name. Add additional branches so that there is one branch for each student. Label each branch with a student's name. Give every student two pieces of green paper and a copy of the leaf pattern on page 88. Instruct each student to use the pattern to trace four leaves and then to cut them out. Then tell her to label each leaf with a description of a special quality that she possesses, such as a talent, skill, or unique character trait. Have the student tack her leaves onto her branch. Do this yourself also, placing your leaves around the trunk of the tree. As the tree foliage blossoms, step back and admire the amazing qualities that crown your classroom!

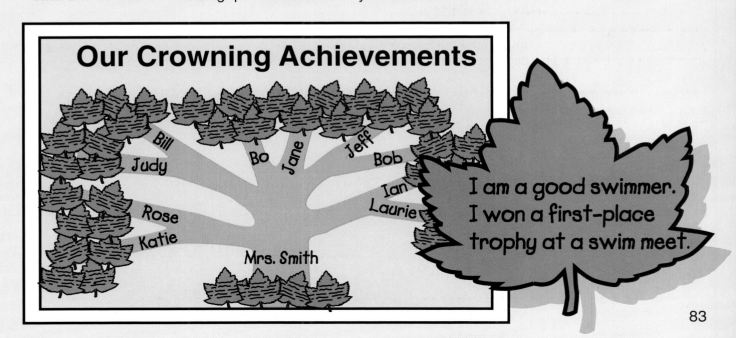

Our Crowning Achievements

Bill
Judy
Bo
Jane
Jeff
Bob
Ian
Laurie
Rose
Katie
Mrs. Smith

I am a good swimmer. I won a first-place trophy at a swim meet.

What's All the Flap About? 🖥

Researching types of trees

There are about 20,000 types of trees in the world. These plants range in size and species from the majestic sequoia towering over 275 feet, to the miniature dwarf tree. Brainstorm with your students a list of trees. Then have each student choose a different type of tree to research. Direct the student to look for the following information: the family to which the tree belongs, its appearance and habitat, its effects on the environment, and the products it produces.

Instruct each student to follow the steps below to create a flap book about his tree. Have the student present his flap book to the rest of the class. Then display the books for all to enjoy.

Directions:

Step 1: Stack three sheets of unlined 8 1/2" x 11" white paper so that the top edges are 1/2" apart.

Step 2: Fold over the top half to form six layers.

Step 3: Staple the book at each side near the top of the fold.

Step 4: Label the front of each flap with a topic title; then write the information on the space above the title so that this information can be seen only by lifting the flap above it.

Step 5: Draw and label an illustration of the tree on the last flap.

Encyclopedia Bound

Researching trees

You're bound to get your kids' interest with this activity! Have your class brainstorm a list of topics to include in an encyclopedia entry on trees. Suggested topics include the importance of trees, types of trees, how trees grow, parts of trees, and tree products. Once the class has established a list of topics, group students into pairs; then assign each pair a topic. Have each pair gather information and take notes on its topic. After students complete their research, instruct each pair to write an encyclopedia entry for its topic on the computer. Organize entries on the computer and use them as a class reference. Encourage students to add new entries as they learn more about trees throughout the year. Another option is to send your entries into cyberspace by publishing them on "Kidopedia Vose." This Internet Web site is an encyclopedia written for kids by kids. The address is http://199.2.210.97/kidopedia.html. Encourage students to add new entries as they learn more about trees throughout the year.

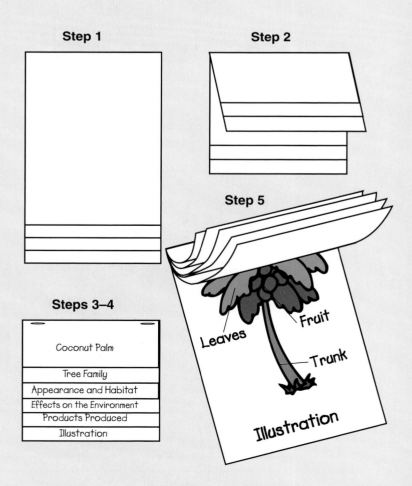

Step 1

Step 2

Steps 3–4

Coconut Palm

Tree Family

Appearance and Habitat

Effects on the Environment

Products Produced

Illustration

Step 5

Leaves

Fruit

Trunk

Illustration

Quilt of Leaves
Observing the characteristics and structure of leaves

Leaves come in a variety of sizes, shapes, and colors. Most leaves are green in spring and summer because of a green pigment called *chlorophyll.* Many leaves have other colors in them also, but these colors are hidden by the green. In late summer and early fall, the chlorophyll breaks down, causing the hidden colors to be revealed. So be it spring, summer, or fall, a tree's vibrant-colored leaves cover the earth much like a beautiful quilt.

Bring this beauty into your classroom by completing the following art activity. Supply each of your students with various colors of 6" x 6" paper (two for each student), several shades of paint, one empty glue bottle for each color of paint, sponges of different shapes, scissors, and glue. Fill each empty glue bottle with a different-colored paint. Have each student gather a variety of leaves from his home or neighborhood. Direct the student to examine the leaves, noting similarities and differences in size, shape, texture, and color. Have the student also observe the leaves' edges and vein patterns.

Invite each student to choose a favorite leaf from his collection. Have him trace his leaf on a piece of colored paper, cut out the leaf, and glue the cutout onto a contrasting-colored square of paper. Next, instruct him to draw the vein pattern onto his paper leaf and then trace the veins using a paint-filled bottle. Finally, have him sponge-paint the background. Post each student's leaf on bulletin board paper to make a colorful quilt of leaves.

Treasures From Trees
Identifying products made from trees

For as long as humans have inhabited the earth, trees have been a source of food, raw material, medicine, and fuel. Have students brainstorm a list of general products made from trees such as wood for fuel, paper, and building materials; cloth; plastics; rubber; turpentine; tannins; and medicines. Discuss the items listed; then tell students to explore their homes tonight to find specific examples of products made from trees. Examples include furniture, Rubbermaid® containers, and wrapping paper. When students return the next day, add the products found at home to the class list.

To help your students visualize the numerous products that trees provide, have your class create a treasure tree. Secure a fallen tree branch in a large container filled with sand or plaster of paris. Give each student a copy of the leaf pattern on page 88 and a piece of green paper. Instruct the student to use the pattern to cut out two leaves and then label each leaf with the name of a product made from trees. Be sure students do not duplicate the names of products. Punch a hole in each of the leaves. Secure them to the tree with yarn, creating a lovely display of tree-given treasures.

Roll 'Em
Understanding the life cycle of a tree, writing for a purpose

A tree is a living organism: It is born, it grows, and it dies. This life cycle begins with a seed falling to the ground. As the seed begins to grow, its root pushes into the soil, and its shoot grows upward toward the sun. Unless the tree becomes diseased or is cut down, it lives for years—providing shade, oxygen, and a home for many creatures. Discuss this life cycle with your students. Then have each student demonstrate his understanding of this cycle by creating a "video book."

Give each student a copy of the video-book pattern on page 89, a copy of the video-strips pattern on page 90, six pieces of 3" x 9" writing paper, one sheet of 9" x 12" construction paper, scissors, a stapler, glue, and crayons. Have each student cut out the video-book pattern, carefully cut slits on lines A and B, and decorate the top right and left squares of the video book. Direct each student to explain the life cycle of a tree by writing each phase of the cycle on a separate sheet of the 3" x 9" paper. Have the student number each page at the top right corner and then staple the pages to the bottom section of his pattern. Next, instruct the student to cut out the video strips, glue them end to end, and sequentially illustrate the life cycle of the tree in the frames. Direct the student to also number each frame in the top right corner so that the illustrations match the corresponding pages. Guide the student to load the book by weaving the video strip from the back up through slit B and then down through slit A. Have each student staple the corners of his video book to the sheet of construction paper; then send him on his way to happy viewing!

The tree keeps growing upward toward the sun.

Something to Talk About
Expressive writing, participating in an oral presentation

About three billion years ago, the first trees appeared on Earth. Today the tallest trees reach more than 30 stories high, and if left undisturbed, live to be hundreds (even thousands) of years old. If trees could talk, imagine the stories they'd tell!

Give trees the opportunity to speak through the voices of your students. To introduce this idea, read *The Big Tree* by Bruce Hiscock. After reading and discussing the story, have students work in pairs to write a skit about an old tree and an interviewer. Tell each pair that the tree is over 100 years old and has seen many things in its life. Have partners decide what type of tree to interview and where it lives. Instruct each pair to create a list of questions to ask the tree that will reveal its life story. For example, have the students ask the tree about people, historical events, other plants and animals, and changes in the environment that have affected the tree's life. After the skits have been written, give each pair the opportunity to practice skit parts with props or costumes. Have each pair perform its skit for the rest of the class.

Just How High? 🖥
Measuring the height of a tree

Your students don't need to climb to the top of a tree to measure its height (even though they may want to)! The height of a tree can be determined with just a few simple tools: a pencil, a notepad, a Popsicle® stick or tongue depressor, a yardstick, and of course a fair-weather day! Take students to an outside area where there are several tall trees, and divide students into pairs. Give each pair a copy of the directions below for finding the height of a tree.

Directions for each pair of students:
1. Choose a tree. Estimate the tree's height. Record your estimate.
2. Student A: Stand by the tree with the Popsicle® stick and the notepad.
3. Student B: Stand directly in front of the tree holding the pencil vertically out in front of you. Back away from the tree with your arm extended, and stop when the pencil and the tree appear to be the same height. Then turn the pencil horizontally, lining up the point of the pencil with the base of the tree trunk.
4. Student B: Instruct student A to move away from the tree until he appears to be standing even with the eraser of the pencil. Instruct him to place the Popsicle® stick in the ground to mark the spot where he is standing.
5. Students A and B: Measure the distance from the base of the tree to the Popsicle® stick. This measurement indicates the height of the tree. Record the length in yards, feet, and inches. How close was your estimate?

Waste Not, Want Not
Understanding conservation, conducting an experiment

Consumers around the world use hundreds of millions of tons of paper each year. That's a lot of trees! Americans have already eliminated 95 percent of all the virgin forests that originally covered the continental United States. How effective is recycling in saving trees? Recycling just one four-foot stack of newspapers saves a 35–40 foot tree! It also saves water and reduces pollution.

Help your students determine how much paper is wasted in the classroom and develop solutions to reduce the amount of paper waste. Direct your class to throw used paper into a box labeled for recycling. At the end of every day, weigh the box to see how much paper has been discarded. At the end of the week, have each student calculate the total amount of paper thrown out (in pounds) and determine a daily average. Brainstorm with your class a list of ways they can conserve paper. The following week put the conservation list into action. Continue to collect recyclable paper, weigh it on a daily basis, and compute the average at the end of the week. After judging the results, determine if more stringent conservation methods are needed, or if your class has become conservation-wise.

A Slice of Life 🖳
Collecting and interpreting data

Counting a tree's growth rings can give a fairly accurate account of its age. The rings also reveal environmental conditions that affect a tree's growth, such as location, drought, flooding, temperature, surrounding foliage, pests, or disease. Fluctuations in these factors affect the width of each growth ring.

Growth occurs every year, in the cell-producing layer of the tree called the *cambium.* This is the area nearest the rough exterior, or *bark.* The next layer, the *sapwood,* is the transportation system of the tree. Water and nutrients flow to the outer branches, leaves, and roots of the tree. The darker *heartwood* is the next layered section that functions as the fortification of the tree. The *pith* is a spongy tissue at the center of these rings that functions mainly in storage.

Visit a local tree-trimming company to obtain several cross-sectional cuts of a tree trunk (enough for small groups of students to observe). As a class, carefully observe one of the cross sections, using it to identify and discuss the functions of each layer of a tree's trunk. Next, divide students into small groups. Give each group a cross section to examine, a ruler, and a copy of page 91. Instruct each group to use the cross section to complete the reproducible. Conclude by having a representative from each group present its data.

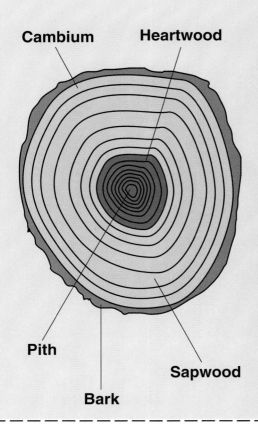

Cambium   **Heartwood**

Pith

Bark

Sapwood

Pattern
Use with "Crowning Achievements" on page 83 and "Treasures From Trees" on page 85.

Pattern
Use this video-book pattern with "Roll 'Em" on page 86.

B   (Cut here.)

A   (Cut here.)

(Staple 3" x 9" paper here.)

Pattern

Use this video-strip pattern with "Roll 'Em" on page 86.

Directions: Cut out the pattern; then separate the strips by cutting along the center dotted line. Glue the right end of the top strip to the left end of the bottom strip.

(Glue here.)

A Slice of Life

Counting a tree's growth rings can tell us much about the age and life of the tree. Use your knowledge of trees, your observation skills, the diagram below, a ruler, and a cross-sectional cut from a tree trunk to help you answer the following questions. Write your answers on the back of this sheet.

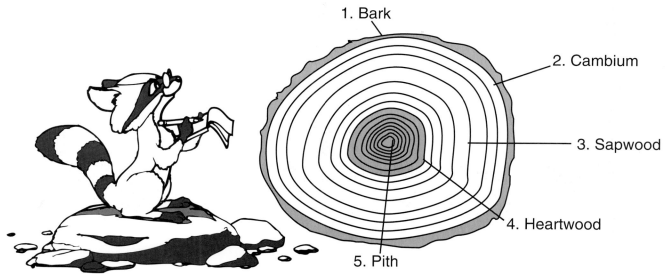

1. Bark
2. Cambium
3. Sapwood
4. Heartwood
5. Pith

1. Determine the age of your tree. Count the number of rings from the center to the outer bark.
2. Using a ruler, measure to see if the center part of the rings, the *pith,* is actually in the center of the trunk. If not, what environmental factors could have made the tree grow toward one side or the other?
3. Measure the diameter of the tree trunk in inches. Be sure that you measure through the center (though not necessarily the pith) of the trunk.
4. Find the *circumference* of the tree by multiplying the diameter by 3.14.
5. Figure the percent of growth for the first ten years of your tree's life by calculating the following:
   - Count the first ten rings from the center ring outward. Count in the direction that shows the most growth.
   - Measure the distance from the center ring to the tenth-year ring.
   - Divide the original diameter in half to find the radius of the tree.
   - Divide the tenth-year ring measure by the radius measure.
   - Round the answer to the nearest hundredth and then express it as a percent by moving the decimal point two places to the right.
6. Use your data to answer the following questions:
   - Are the rings of the tree all the same size?
   - What might account for the differences in ring widths?
   - Are trees with the same diameter necessarily the same age? Why or why not?

Bonus Box: Write a paragraph that tells the life story of your tree. Base the imagined events of your tree's life on the clues revealed by the number, shape, and size of your tree's rings.

Answer Keys

Page 32

1. Day 11

Day	1	2	3	4	5	6	7	8	9	10	11				
Number of Sit-Ups	20	23	26	29	32	35	38	41	44	47	50				

2. 27 choices

blue shirt with black shorts and striped towel
blue shirt with black shorts and solid-colored towel
blue shirt with black shorts and checked towel
blue shirt with gray shorts and striped towel
blue shirt with gray shorts and solid-colored towel
blue shirt with gray shorts and checked towel
blue shirt with brown shorts and striped towel
blue shirt with brown shorts and solid-colored towel
blue shirt with brown shorts and checked towel

red shirt with black shorts and striped towel
red shirt with black shorts and solid-colored towel
red shirt with black shorts and checked towel
red shirt with gray shorts and striped towel
red shirt with gray shorts and solid-colored towel
red shirt with gray shorts and checked towel
red shirt with brown shorts and striped towel
red shirt with brown shorts and solid-colored towel
red shirt with brown shorts and checked towel

white shirt with black shorts and striped towel
white shirt with black shorts and solid-colored towel
white shirt with black shorts and checked towel
white shirt with gray shorts and striped towel
white shirt with gray shorts and solid-colored towel
white shirt with gray shorts and checked towel
white shirt with brown shorts and striped towel
white shirt with brown shorts and solid-colored towel
white shirt with brown shorts and checked towel

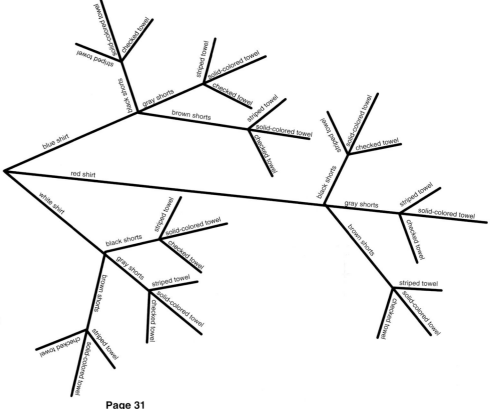

3. Alan walked.

	Alan	Jeremy	Trevor
Traveled By Car	✕	✓	✕
Walked	✓	✕	✕
Rode a Bicycle	✕	✕	✓

4. There were six bicycles in the shop.

Number of Tricycles	Number of Tricycle Wheels	Number of Bicycles	Number of Bicycle Wheels	Total Number of Cycles	Total Number of Wheels
1	3	17	34	18	37
2	6	16	32	18	38
3	9	15	30	18	39
4	12	14	28	18	40
5	15	13	26	18	41
6	18	12	24	18	42
7	21	11	22	18	43
8	24	10	20	18	44
9	27	9	18	18	45
10	30	8	16	18	46
11	33	7	14	18	47
12	36	6	12	18	48

Page 31

Accept questions written with different wording that reflects the students' general understanding of the terms.

1. *decimal number;* What is the name for a fractional number that is written with a decimal point?
2. *dividend;* What is a number that is to be divided in a division problem?
3. *prime number;* What is a number whose only factors are one and itself?
4. *perimeter;* What is the distance around the outside of a closed figure?
5. *square;* What is a rectangle with congruent sides?
6. *symmetric;* What is a figure with two halves that are reflections of one another?
7. *factor;* What is one of the numbers that are multiplied to find a product?
8. *graph;* What is a drawing that shows the relationships between sets of numbers?
9. *congruent angles;* What are angles that have the same measure?
10. *rhombus;* What is a parallelogram with congruent sides?

Bonus Box: Alphabetical order: *eight, five, four, nine, one, seven, six, three, two, zero.*

Page 33

1. 0.6 = GO
2. 8078 = BLOB
3. 618 = BIG
4. 7738 = BELL
5. 607 = LOG
6. 7714 = HILL
7. 3507 = LOSE
8. 38076 = GLOBE
9. A. 7105 = SOIL
   B. 7716 = GILL
10. A. 7718 = BILL
    B. 3045 = SHOE

Page 58
1. 4—Puerto Rico Trench
   3—Diamantina Depth
   5—Mariana Trench
   2—Aleutian Trench
   1—Cayman Trench

2. 23,000 ft.
   25,000 ft.
   26,000 ft.
   28,000 ft.
   36,000 ft.

3. and 4.

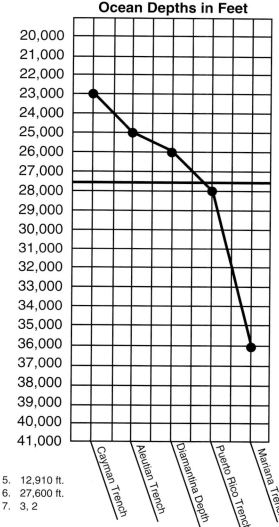

Ocean Depths in Feet

5. 12,910 ft.
6. 27,600 ft.
7. 3, 2

Page 67
1. Wrens—Peters, Cats—Young
2. 3
3. Smith
4. 3
5. Wrens, 5–2
6. 9
7. Brady, Smith
8. 7
9. Two hours and 59 minutes
10. 38,086

Page 68

Spinner One
1. 1/3
2. 2/3
3. Answers will vary.
4. Answers will vary.
5. Answers will vary.
6. Answers will vary.

Spinner Two
1. 1/6
2. 5/6
3. Answers will vary.
4. Answers will vary.
5. Answers will vary.
6. Answers will vary.

Page 78
1. 10 pennies, 4 dimes, 2 quarters
2. 15 pennies, 9 nickels, 4 dimes
3. 15 pennies, 7 nickels, 2 quarters
4. 3 nickels, 6 dimes, 1 quarter
5. 10 pennies, 2 nickels, 3 dimes, 2 quarters
6. 10 pennies, 3 nickels, 5 dimes, 1 quarter

Page 80
Answers will vary.
Bonus Box: The total value of the entire alphabet is $351.00.

Page 81
1. *The Sun*—$6.00, *The Evening Post*—$5.70
2. *The Evening Post*
3. *The Sun*—$10.00, *The Evening Post*—$7.75
4. $17.75
5. *The Sun*—$15.00, *The Evening Post*—$10.75
6. $25.75
7. *The Sun*—$14.00, *The Evening Post*—$10.85
8. *The Evening Post*

Bonus Box: Answers will vary.

Page 82
If each person eats one of each menu item, the chart will look like this:

Item	Cost	# Needed	Subtotal	Item	Cost	# Needed	Subtotal
Hot Dogs (8-pack)	$2.50	3	$7.50	Paper Plates (25 count)	$1.99	1	$1.99
Hot Dog Buns (12-pack)	$0.99	2	$1.98	Napkins (100 count)	$0.99	1	$0.99
Coca-Cola® (6-pack)	$1.19	4	$4.76	Ketchup, 16 oz.	$1.19	1	$1.19
Doritos® (case of 24 small bags)	$5.99	1	$5.99	Mustard, 12 oz.	$1.09	1	$1.09
Cupcakes (1 dozen)	$2.59	2	$5.18	**Grand Total** (not including tax)			$30.67
				Cost Per Person			$1.28

93

Index